Dennis Johnson has done it again in his coverage of the fundamentals of modern campaigning from raising money to communicating with voters and measuring public opinion to identifying voters and turning them out on Election Day. More important, however, is his examination of innovative new techniques and new developments in these fundamental areas from online tools like social networks and the use of "big data" to the importance of Super PACs and micro-targeting. *Campaigning in the Twenty-First Century* is a must-read for anyone interested in the most current trends in American campaigning.

David Dulio, *Oakland University*

Dennis Johnson does a great job of explaining how communications technology and data analytics have transformed modern campaigning. In a clear, concise manner, he shows how the fundamental role of campaigns has remained while the tactics have changed—and in a way that invites citizens to engage in politics directly. This book will help anyone with an interest in campaigns understand what is going on in the world of politics today.

Robin Kolodny, *Temple University*

The second edition of *Campaigning in the Twenty-First Century* sets a new standard for understanding the electoral process in the modern era. It is overflowing with astute insights on how the dynamics of the election process play out in the American context. I cannot recommend this book strongly enough.

Brian Frederick, *Bridgewater State University*

Dennis Johnson pulls back the curtain on a process—election campaigning—that simultaneously fascinates and baffles most citizens. In *Campaigning in the Twenty-First Century*, Johnson uses important historical examples and draws upon the latest scholarship to explain how every element of a campaign operates. Those who want to understand American political campaigns should start by reading this book.

Stephen K. Medvic, *Franklin & Marshall College*

Campaigning in the Twenty-First Century takes a scholarly, methodical approach to the whiz-bang world of electoral politics. Examining the recent history of campaign technology and organization, Johnson reveals the state of the art—and anticipates the future. This book is sure to help scholars, practitioners, and students better understand one of the central forces driving American democracy.

Michael Burton, *Ohio University*

Campaigning in the Twenty-First Century

This thoroughly revised second edition looks at the extraordinary changes that have occurred in American campaigns since the beginning of the twenty-first century. Dennis W. Johnson looks at the most sophisticated techniques of modern campaigning—micro-targeting, online fundraising, digital communication, the new media—and examines what has changed, how those changes have dramatically transformed campaigning, and what has remained fundamentally the same despite new technologies and forms of communication.

Twenty-first century campaigns, particularly at the presidential level, have seen extraordinary growth in the involvement of outside groups, Super PACs, and special interest money. Federal campaign finance laws have become eviscerated and unreported "dark" money has poured into campaigns. Activists have flexed their political muscle, advancing their causes through social media and old-fashioned door-to-door hustle. *Campaigning in the Twenty-First Century* presents daunting challenges for candidates and professional consultants as they try to get their messages out to voters. Ironically, the more open and robust campaigns become, the greater is the need for seasoned, flexible and imaginative professional consultants.

Dennis W. Johnson is Professor Emeritus of political management and former Associate Dean at the Graduate School of Political Management, George Washington University.

Also by the author

Political Consultants and American Elections, Third Edition (2015)
(formerly **No Place for Amateurs**)

The Laws that Shaped America
Fifteen Acts of Congress and Their Lasting Impact (2009)

Congress Online
Bridging the Gap Between Citizens and
Their Representatives (2004)

Co-editor, **Campaigning for President 2016: Strategy and Tactics**
(forthcoming, 2017)

Editor, **Campaigning for President 2012: Strategy and Tactics** (2013)

Editor, **Campaigning for President 2008**
Strategy and Tactics, New Voices and New Techniques (2009)

Editor, **The Routledge Handbook of Political Management** (2009)

All published by Routledge

Campaigning in the Twenty-First Century

Activism, Big Data, and Dark Money

Second Edition

Dennis W. Johnson

Routledge
Taylor & Francis Group

NEW YORK AND LONDON

Second edition published 2016
by Routledge
711 Third Avenue, New York, NY 10017

and by Routledge
2 Park Square, Milton Park, Abingdon, Oxon, OX14 4RN

Routledge is an imprint of the Taylor & Francis Group, an informa business

First edition published by Routledge 2011

Library of Congress Cataloging in Publication Data
A catalog record for this book has been requested

ISBN: 9781138122192 (hbk)
ISBN: 9781138122208 (pbk)
ISBN: 9781315650586 (ebk)

Typeset in Garamond
by Cenveo Publisher Services

Printed and bound in the United States of America by Publishers Graphics,
LLC on sustainably sourced paper.

For Pat, with all my love

Contents

Tables

Preface

Professional political campaigning has undergone dramatic, even fundamental, changes over the past decade; yet many of the tried and true practices found in the twentieth century remain valuable tools today. The crowded field of Republican and Democratic candidates for the 2016 presidential nomination rely on old-fashioned rallies, fund raising events, and television ads to get their message across as they try to woo voters. Candidates have been doing this for generations. We can reliably call these activities twentieth century campaigning. But the 2016 candidates have also turned to Twitter, trying to reach supporters and grab the attention of traditional media. The candidates have also turned to outside funding sources, Super PACs and 501(c) groups, to fuel their campaigns and to help sustain them through the primaries and ultimately through the general election. In that way, the 2016 candidates are definitely using twenty-first century campaigning techniques.

Twenty-first century campaigning started nearly twenty years ago. There is no specific beginning point, but if we were to locate one nascent moment, it would have been an announcement made on television. On Thursday evening, October 6, 1996, PBS host Jim Lehrer moderated the first of three presidential debates between incumbent Bill Clinton and Republican challenger Bob Dole. The debate itself at the Bushnell Theater in Hartford, Connecticut was unremarkable and not very news worthy. But in his closing arguments, Bob Dole did something that no other major party candidate had done: he invited the millions of viewers to find out more about the Dole-Kemp campaign and to join its efforts by logging on to his campaign website.

> I ask for your support. I ask for your help. And if you really want to get involved, just tap into my home page, www.DoleKemp96org. Thank you. God bless America.[1]

Dole bungled the URL address, forgetting the "dot" before "org," but the next day there were well over 2 million hits on his campaign's website. Neither the Dole-Kemp nor the Clinton-Gore campaign website was very sophisticated, amounting to little more than bulletin boards for campaign promises and statements. But they attracted attention and helped welcome in the age of online political communication.

The 1996 presidential contest was dominated by what we might call twentieth century campaigning: television advertising was the principal medium of communication, along with radio ads, direct mail, and telephone banks, all orchestrated by political consultants who embraced a top-down approach to strategy and decision making. This twentieth century model of professional consulting and campaigning evolved over the years, and began taking root in presidential, gubernatorial, and U.S. Senate campaigns during the mid-1960s. But starting in 1996, we were about to enter a new era, a period of rapid change in technology, in online communications, and perhaps fundamentally, in how citizens interacted with candidates and, even more significantly, how citizens interacted with one another. We were about to enter twenty-first century campaigning. For many election cycles thereafter, scholars, pundits and election watchers have predicted extraordinary, transformational, changes in the way campaigns would operate. Indeed, the 2012 and 2016 presidential campaigns and recent mid-term elections, in many ways, have shown how far we have come in changing the landscape of electioneering.

Many of the changes we have seen since 1996 have been in response to the revolution in online technology, from email, Internet, social networking, and micro-blogging. There have also been profound changes in the technology of data base management, digital images, and the like. But not all campaign changes have come about because of technological improvements. For example, a major development at the federal election level (presidential, U.S. Senate and House of Representatives) came when the campaign finance law was significantly modified in 2002, and then changed even more profoundly following an important Supreme Court decision in 2010.

In this book, I try to answer several important questions: With all the changes in technology and communication, how have campaigns and citizens been affected? In what ways have the fundamentals of professional campaigning remained the same? While the impulse is toward change, in many ways campaigns have not changed that much at all.

This book focuses on professionally run campaigns held since 2000. Most of our attention is on candidate campaigns, such as gubernatorial, congressional, or presidential contests in the United States. But the findings and observations could apply equally to ballot initiatives, local elections, and to a growing number of international campaigns as well. Since 1996, there have been six presidential election cycles, hundreds of gubernatorial contests, hundreds more of U.S. Senate elections, several thousand congressional contests, and countless local elections that have been big enough to employ professional consultants.

New to the Second Edition

Several important changes have occurred in American elections since the publication of the first edition of this book. The most visible change has come in the financing of federal elections. With the experience of the 2012 presidential election, the congressional elections of 2010, 2012, and 2014, and now the 2016 presidential cycle, we are seeing the ramifications of the Supreme Court's *Citizens United* decision. That decision, along with other court rulings, has nearly eviscerated federal campaign laws. When soft money was banned, campaigns and advocacy groups turned to 527 organizations, which now have been supplanted by politically active 501(c) social welfare organizations and Super PACs. The long-standing rule that campaign money must be disclosed is now circumvented by so-called "dark money," and mega-donors, shelling out millions of dollars, are resetting the balance of campaigns. The Koch brothers, Sheldon Adelson, and George Soros are joined by other wealthy donors trying to defeat or elect candidates. Unaffiliated Super PACs, often with innocuous-sounding names, mobilize ground troops and through their hard-hitting ads become the "hit men" of the campaign, doing the dirty work for the candidates they support. The other long-standing rule on contribution limits has also been brushed aside. As a result of this Wild West of freely flowing and often unreported money, federal campaigns have skyrocketed in costs, and in many cases more money has come in from outside groups than from the candidate campaigns themselves.

We have also seen, especially through the Obama 2012 re-election campaign, a growing sophistication in the use of Big Data and technology. What was novel in 2008 became standard practice in 2012, and more importantly became thoroughly integrated into campaign tactics. Algorithms and analytics in many ways supplanted practices considered state of the art just a few cycles ago. We learned about these techniques from Project Narwhal and Project Orca, the Optimizer, and the Obama dashboard during the 2012 presidential cycle.

As we will see in this edition, television is still the dominant medium but is being challenged by a variety of online sources, cable television users can now be micro-targeted with a considerable degree of sophistication. We'll see the explosion in social media and its impact on campaigns, and how the growing use of cell phones continues to challenge pollsters. New players have come on to the scene, from Ted Cruz, Donald Trump, Chris Christie, and Ben Carson among those vying for the 2016 Republican nomination; and candidates of all stripes are facing new challenges and hurdles as they try to convince an increasingly skeptical and fragmented voting public.

Politics, campaigning, candidates, technology, and communication do not stand still. And in this completely revised second edition we will see some significant changes in the dynamics of campaigning in the twenty-first century.

In Chapter 1, I survey the requirements for solid competitive campaigns, from the presidential level, through statewide contests, to local contests. In many ways, the requirements are the same—raising money, communicating with voters, getting them out to the polling stations, but within this fundamental framework, there is a considerable variation on what services and practices constitute the modern professionally run campaign. In addition, I introduce a twenty-first century model of campaigning.

The following chapters discuss these essential elements in a successful campaign and how they have changed over the past decade. Chapters 2 and 3 look at the critical role of communicating with voters. In Chapter 2, I examine the New Media—email, websites, web videos, mobile phones, social network sites, twittering, blogging, and other recent online phenomena. In Chapter 3, I look at the still critical role of Old Media—particularly television and direct mail. Chapter 4 concerns the important role of raising money. Chapter 5 examines the vital role of survey research and measuring public opinion, while Chapter 6 focuses on the importance of identifying, targeting and getting voters out to the polling stations. Chapter 7 looks at the growing influence of outside voices in campaigns and how they have developed over time. Finally in Chapter 8, I give my best guess (and those of professional consultants and election analysts) as to what changes might be coming in the next decade of professional campaigning.

I have interviewed a number of political consultants and other experts in elections and campaigning and I thank them for their cooperation and frank assessments. Further, I have drawn on the growing scholarly literature on campaigns and elections, professionally run campaigns and applied politics.

While so much has changed in professional campaigning, much still remains the same. Many tried and true methods of campaigning have been refined and updated, and in order to survive, consulting teams have adapted new methods and techniques. Through this book I have explored both the new and the old, have given a glimpse at future campaigning, and given a sense of the dynamics of campaigning in the twenty-first century.

My thanks to my faculty colleagues, students, and alumni of the Graduate School of Political Management at George Washington University. My thanks to senior editor Jennifer Knerr and senior editorial assistant Ze'ev Sudry at Routledge, along with the production editor Carrie Bell.

Dennis W. Johnson
Chatham, Massachusetts

1　The Modern Campaign

Congrats@LindseyGrahamSC. You just got 4 points in your home state of SC—far better than zero nationally. You're only 26 pts behind me.
—Donald Trump tweet, August 25, 2015;
@realDonaldTrump

So while Hillary Clinton and John McCain set out to run the last campaign all over again, [Barack] Obama forged ahead and ran the first campaign of the twenty-first century.
—Garrett M. Graff (2009)

The [Scott] Brown campaign employed iPhone apps, YouTube videos, hashtags and Facebook to turn a long-shot, shoestring campaign into a much broader political movement. [Martha] Coakley, says Rob Willington, Brown's social-media strategist, never knew what she was up against. "We ran circles around her," he says, "It was incredible."
—Sophia Yan, *Time* (2010)

It was an operatic fall from power, swift and deep and utterly surprising. As late as Tuesday morning, [Eric] Cantor had felt so confident of victory that he spent the morning at a Starbuck's on Capitol Hill, holding a fund-raising meeting with lobbyists while his constituents went to the polls.
—*Washington Post* (2014)

On election night in November 2008, Chicago's Grant Park was brimming with excitement and electricity, as Barack Obama ascended the stage to acknowledge the hundreds of thousands of well-wishers and to give his first speech as president-elect. The spectacle was beamed world wide as billions of television viewers caught a glimpse of the new president and his family. To many, the presidential election was a powerful sign of America's strength as a democratic nation; many others undoubtedly were perplexed and perhaps bemused by the long, complicated, and expensive theatrics of electoral politics. For those who follow elections and professional consulting closely, the Obama campaign was the best financed, best run, and most sophisticated combination of online technology, social networking and grassroots activism, and blending of new and old media. It was the envy of the campaign world, soon to be copied and emulated by Republicans and Democrats, other aspirants for high office, and campaigns throughout the world.

Just over fourteen months later, on Tuesday evening, January 19, 2010, another jubilant crowd assembled at the Park Plaza Hotel in Boston, cheering the improbable victory of state legislator Scott Brown, who captured the U.S. Senate seat long held by Edward M. Kennedy. Brown won with a clear message of opposition to national health care, his good looks and pickup truck, a lackluster opponent, and the anger and energy of antigovernment activists. It was a campaign ready-made for online activism. Campaign insiders looked at the Brown race and the crushing Republican victories in the 2010 mid-term elections and discovered how much further down the road of social networking and online communication they had come, using techniques that were just beginning to be developed by the Obama presidential campaign.

In June 2014, another improbable victory occurred in a Virginia Republican primary election battle. House majority leader Eric Cantor and his consultants completely misread the challenge coming from little-known economics professor David Brat. Fueled by Tea Party anger and distrust, Brat decisively beat Cantor. Brat supporters used social media and old-fashioned door-to-door hustle to bring out disaffected Republicans. Cantor had the overwhelming financial edge, the experienced political consultants, and name recognition, but none of this could overcome a determined opposition. Too few of Cantor's supporters came to the polls, and the wrath of the Tea Party sent shivers throughout the Republican establishment.

Political campaign strategies and techniques have evolved and transformed. What was new and creative in 2000 was surpassed in 2004; what was exciting and unique in 2008 has been improved upon in 2016. But it isn't just greater emphasis on social media or data mining technologies that have transformed campaigning. It is also the impact of unregulated funds, "dark money," that has made campaigning far more expensive, the anger and activism of citizens fed up with government gridlock, and the role played by plutocrats, willing to pour millions of dollars into national and state elections. Over this past decade, a new model of professional political campaigning has been emerging: one that is far less top-down controlled by political consultants, has greater engagement of ordinary citizens, and is fueled by the ease and access of online communication. What has been emerging is the twenty-first century model of campaigning.

Twentieth Century Campaign Model

For most of American history, from the mid-1820s through the first half of the twentieth century, campaigning was dominated by the political parties. The parties recruited candidates, made campaign funds available, assessed public opinion, and mobilized voters for the elections.[1] By the 1960s, however, the political parties had lost their hold on electioneering and individual candidates began to hire their own teams of experts, political consultants and operatives. This became known as the era of the candidate-centered election. Candidates were often on their own: responsible for raising their own campaign funds, hiring their own consultants and campaign team, and running their own race independently of the party. The connection with their political party was sometimes so tenuous that candidates would not even mention their party affiliation in campaign advertisements and literature. By the late 1960s and early 1970s, political consultants routinely began working for individual candidates, and in the last two decades of the twentieth century, they became permanent fixtures in American elections.

A look at a competitive, well-funded U.S. Senate campaign in 1990, for example, would show the extent to which candidates relied on professional assistance. The candidate would hire a full range of political consultants and campaign operatives: a campaign manager, media team, private pollster, researchers, fundraisers, voter identification, targeting and get-out-the-vote specialists, direct mail and telephone operations. In order to pay for the consultants, the polling, phone bank, television advertising, direct mail expenditures, staff and office expenditures, and countless others, the campaign would need to raise approximately $5 million.

This typical campaign, and thousands of others like it, illustrates the twentieth century model of campaigning.

First, political consultants were in a command-and-control mode. They would be the dominant voice in defining the contest, creating strategy, and in maintaining message discipline (or in consultant James Carville's well-remembered words from the 1992 Clinton presidential campaign, "It's the economy, stupid!"). Candidates, of course, would have the last word and were ultimately responsible for the conduct and tone of their campaign, but often the decisions were driven by the experience and knowledge of the senior consultants. The campaign manager, a general consultant, the pollster, the media team, perhaps the direct mail specialists, would join the trusted political allies or senior political staff of the candidate to craft the message and plot strategy. Much of what consultants did was based on past campaigns, their own instincts and creativity.

Second, the consultants and strategist would employ a top-down method of communicating. They would gather information from likely voters, be guided by survey research results through polls, focus groups and dial meter sessions, but would not involve individual voters or activists in the critical decisions of the campaign, such as, what the candidate says, the shape and content of the candidate's television commercials, where the candidate goes, what issues are important and should be emphasized. Consultants were in control, and knew that without their discipline and determination, the inherent chaos of an election could drive them into a ditch.

Third, campaigns relied on television as the chief medium of communication. For many secondary races in major media markets which could not afford television, direct mail became the communication weapon of choice. Campaigns also relied on radio advertising, bill boards, phone banks, and news print to get their message across to likely voters.

Fourth, campaigns had time to craft messages, days and even weeks to put together television advertising, time to absorb an opponent's attack and then to respond in kind. Campaigns would follow news cycles, which meant the morning drive-time, noon day news, and evening news at 6:00 p.m. and late news coverage at 10:00 or 11:00 p.m. With the advent of all-news television and radio channels and 24/7 news cycles, campaign messaging and communication were compelled to go on all-day and all-night alert. Polling results, which in earlier times took days to analyze and report, became more readily available, and their analyses was aided by advances in software technology.

Fifth, much of the campaign was based on guesswork, instinct, and past experience. Campaigns had polling numbers and cross-tabulations, but could only guess whether a television commercial or direct mail advertisement might be effective. Campaigns relied on past voting data and census figures, and were just beginning to factor in other elements, such as lifestyle choices, intensity of support for issues or candidates, or other matters.

Sixth, fundraising was conducted primarily through big ticket events, where a small number of contributors would "max out," give the largest amount of money permitted by law. Direct mail was the vehicle of choice for reaching those contributors who gave less money, but it was very expensive to cast about for potential donors. Small-dollar donations, $25 or so, were also received, but it was difficult and expensive to rely on such small givers. Except for special events, it was very hard to raise large amounts of money in short periods of time.

Seventh, except in presidential and other high-profile campaigns, voters were basically spectators. They would be asked primarily to do one thing, show up on election day and cast their ballot. Few voters contributed money, volunteered on campaigns, or interacted with the campaign in any way.

The Online Revolution

The twentieth century model prevailed during the 1960s through the 1990s, and in many campaigns, particularly those less well funded, has extended to the present time. But then came the online revolution.

Since before the turn into this century, political analysts and online communications advocates had been arguing that the Internet, email, and other forms of online communications would transform politics and electioneering. Pioneering candidates and campaigns in America had used the Internet and email since the mid-1990s, and by the presidential race of 2000, these tools became integral parts of the most successful candidate communication activities. By 2000, one could probably sum up the use of online communication as still a work in progress. Remember, this was years before Facebook, YouTube, blogging, smartphones, Twitter, or a whole host of social media tools. By the 2008 presidential election, online communication had truly come into it own as significant campaign tool.[2]

As seen in Chapter 2, online campaigning has changed dramatically since Bob Dole announced his website address during the 1996 debates. In those early days, campaign websites were static, often merely political bulletin boards giving viewers little more than electronic versions of the campaign's literature.[3] Two candidates and their consultants stood out in the use of this new technology. First, was Jesse Ventura, a third-party candidate for governor of Minnesota in 1998. This former U.S. Navy Seal and professional wrestler improbably won in a three-way race, appealing particularly to young people, many of whom never voted before, attracting them through his fledgling website. The second was the 2000 campaign of Senator John S. McCain III of Arizona for the Republican nomination for president. McCain was able to raise over $2 million in just two days through his campaign website. When that remarkable amount of money, mostly in small donations, poured into the McCain campaign, rival candidates and consultants began to take seriously the potential of online communications.

During the 2004 presidential campaign, online communication and campaigning arrived at a new plateau. By this time, campaigns had learned to create fairly sophisticated websites and they were about to exploit other aspects of online communication. Senator John Edwards of North Carolina announced his candidacy for the Democratic nomination through his website. Congressman Dennis Kucinich of Ohio, with little money and name recognition, heavily relied on the Internet and online communication to appeal to voters. Online activists were becoming factors as well. For example, there was a strong push by groups formed online to persuade retired U.S. Army general Wesley Clark to enter the race for the Democratic nomination, and, encouraged by this support, Clark declared his candidacy.

However, the best use of online communication during the 2004 presidential primaries came from the campaign of Howard Dean, former governor of Vermont, who was running for the Democratic nomination.[4] While Dean himself was not adept at online communication, his staff, particularly campaign manager Joe Trippi, ventured into new online strategies. The Dean campaign gave us three innovations: First, was interactive communication between supporters and the campaign. Dean became the first presidential candidate to create a blog (called Blog for America), and the first to employ a blogmaster as a paid employee of his campaign. The campaign encouraged supporters to participate, give advice, suggest campaign ideas, and come up with policy options. Even more, Dean promised to take the best ideas and incorporate them into his campaign. This was a revolutionary approach to running a campaign: rather than rely on the traditional top-down, message-disciplined campaign run by professionals, Dean promised to listen to his supporters and act according to their wishes. Yet when actual votes had to be counted, the energetic Dean grassroots-online campaign famously crashed in the Iowa caucus. Other presidential candidates, however, saw the value and promise of online communication, and began creating their own blogs.

Second, the Dean campaign was particularly adept at gathering together supporters and volunteers, reaching them through online communication. The campaign collaborated with Meetup.com, a website that encouraged like-minded persons to come together. This was social networking in its infancy, in the days before Facebook and other sites caught on in the political arena. By July 1, 2003, seven months before the Iowa caucus, the Dean campaign had gathered 49,260 individuals through Meetup.com; by the time of the Iowa caucus, in February 2004, Dean had signed up 187,525 supporters through his website.

The third innovation was online fundraising. While McCain four years earlier had raised a few million dollars online, the Dean campaign raised $41 million, mostly from small-amount donors who gave between $25 and $100 each. In past presidential contests, only relatively few Americans actually contributed money. In the 2000 presidential primaries, for example, just 770,000 individuals, out of a total adult population of 185 million, gave funds. Dean's innovation was to expand this pool, using the convenience of the Internet, to reach hundreds of thousands of new donors.

The exhilaration of the Dean campaign, with its fundraising triumphs, its Meetup house parties, and fervent volunteers, quickly faded, however, when Dean lost in the Iowa caucus. While hundreds of Dean volunteers scoured Iowa, the campaign had failed to make a real connection with those who counted the most—the hard-core Iowa Democrats who show up, election after election, for party caucuses. In trying to woo savvy and knowledgeable Iowa Democrats, the three frontrunner candidates with the most at stake in Iowa—John Kerry, Richard Gephardt, and Howard Dean—poured millions of dollars into television advertising, that old reliable medium of communication.

During the 2004 presidential election, the Internet and online communication proved to be powerful and relatively inexpensive mechanisms for gathering supporters, sharing ideas, and collecting funds. But these online tools could not work magic. Internet-dependent candidates like Dennis Kucinich and Wesley Clark, without the charisma and sharply pointed ideas of Dean, went nowhere. Online communication seems an ideal mechanism for exciting candidates, with fiercely loyal supporters, who were poised to bring about the next political revolution. Yet ironically, probably the best use of the Internet and email communication during this election came from the most traditional of sources, the Bush-Cheney re-election campaign. As Mike McCurry, former spokesman for President Bill Clinton and consultant for the Kerry 2004 campaign, noted, "We ran the last best campaign of the twentieth century. Republicans began what it takes to run campaigns in the twenty-first century."[5]

The 2008 presidential campaign offered us the most technologically savvy presidential candidate, Barack Obama. Armed with his two Blackberrys, Obama first had to do battle against Hillary Clinton, who announced her candidacy over the Internet but then ran a much more traditional twentieth century campaign, and in the general election, against John McCain, who didn't even use email and whose campaign used some of the bells and whistles of online communication, but not with the same remarkable effects as Obama. As seen in more detail in Chapter 2, the Obama campaign set the standard for the use of online technology, the integration of offline and online elements, and innovative usage of social media, cell phones, and television.

Obama campaign manager David Plouffe stated that technology "was core to our campaign from Day One and it only grew in importance."[6] The campaign invested heavily in staff and equipment. Digital campaign veterans from the Howard Dean campaign, like Joe Rospars and Jascha Franklin-Hodge, both of whom then worked for Blue State Digital, Chris Hughes who along with Mark Zuckerberg had co-founded Facebook. com, and a number of executives from technology companies teamed up to form the backbone of the online campaign team. Nearly ninety staffers were hired, and millions were spent on servers, email systems, web development, and text messaging. A single database, with terabytes of information, was created, integrating all aspects of fundraising, social networking, and activism from MyBarackObama.com—something never done before in presidential campaigns.[7]

Aided by online communication, Obama supporters held more than 100,000 events throughout the country; more than 10,000 persons applied to become one of the 3,000 Obama "organizing fellows" who would go out into their communities to register voters; and more than 3 million phone calls were made by Obama supporters during the last four days of the campaign alone.[8]

The Obama campaign raised more money than any other candidate had in history, much of it from small-amount donors online. As seen in Chapter 4, some 3 million people made 6.5 million donations to the Obama campaign, an equally unprecedented number of donors and unprecedented amount of contributions.

The Obama campaign used cell phone text messaging at rallies and large events, particularly encouraging supporters to text the campaign to learn about Obama's vice-presidential selection of Senator Joe Biden. As a result, the campaign now had millions of cell phone numbers that could be used to text messages. By contrast, during its campaign, the McCain forces sent only one text message, a reminder the day before the election for supporters to vote.[9]

The Obama campaign oversaw more than 100 different websites, had fifty-seven different profiles on MySpace, created nearly 2,000 YouTube videos, including the most successful YouTube entry, Obama's thirty-seven-minute speech on race in Philadelphia during the 2008 primary season, which was watched by more people online than seen on television.

What the Obama team had done could have been done by any of the twenty major party candidates for president that year. There was nothing radically new about the technology; there was no secret formula. The key was the integration of online campaigning into the overall campaign: in fundraising, field organizing, and communications. Garrett M. Graff, a veteran of the Dean presidential bid, observed that "the game-changer in the Obama campaign ... was that technology and the Internet was not an add-on for them. It was a carefully considered element of almost every critical campaign function."[10]

Technology and social media integration were ramped up even more during the 2012 presidential election. While the Romney campaign made significant strides beyond the McCain effort in 2008, it still lagged behind the Obama re-election campaign. The key to the Obama success was the integration of technologies, increased use of social media, aggressive use of online advertising and mobile phone apps. This will be discussed further in the following chapter.

The Scott Brown campaign for the Massachusetts U.S. Senate seat in early 2010 had to overcome several major obstacles: the state was over-whelmingly Democratic; voters were asked to replace the liberal icon, Edward M. Kennedy who had served since 1962; and Brown was far behind state attorney general Martha Coakley, a Democrat, in fundraising and name recognition. Yet Brown upset Coakley, who had run a fairly tradi-tional, but also lackluster campaign. Brown tapped into the anger and resentment of Massachusetts voters, and during just a few months was able to use online video and social networking to stir up and energize support-ers. In the last few weeks of the campaign, Brown campaign videos received more than 500,000 hits on YouTube (compared to just 51,000 views for

Coakley). His social media presence on Facebook was ten times that of his opponent. Using Ning, a social platform, the Brown campaign, under its social-media strategist Rob Willington, created the "Brown Brigade," a network that easily connected the campaign to grassroot supporters. Brown also had 10,000 people following him on Twitter and 76,000 fans on Facebook. In a fundraising blitz, the Brown campaign raised $1.3 million in one day, using this social networking site. The campaign also relied heavily on text messaging and on advertising on Google.[11]

Twenty-First Century Campaign Model

In comparison with the most forward thinking election campaigns in 2014 or 2016, those of fifteen years earlier on the surface may seem antiquated. With the online revolution, it seems like a whole new ballgame for candidates, political consultants, political activists, and voters. The reality is, however, more complicated. A new campaign model is emerging, but in many ways it still fits into the contours of the twentieth century model.

First, political consultants will still dominate in defining the contest, setting its objectives, and laying out the strategy for victory. Consultants, in fact, will be in much greater demand because of the greater possibility of chaos and uncertainty. With many more voices involved, with greater online and old media clutter, the more there is the need for a clear, determined voice to define the race and state the case for the candidate. Campaigns will forever need to focus on fundraising, developing and communicating their message, and mobilizing voters and getting them to vote. Campaigns in the twenty-first century model will rely heavily on campaign managers, general consultants, pollsters, media team, direct mail and other specialists. What will change, however, is the acceptance and the integration of online media and technology into the core of the campaign. As the online component of campaigning began to mature, campaigns realized the importance of having a webmaster, a blog specialist, a director of social media, an online advertising group, an online staff with equal strategic importance as any other component of the campaign. Ultimately, in the best-run campaigns, the online component will be a seamless, integral part of all campaign functions.

Second, the top-down, command-and-control model will give way to a more fluid model, which encourages citizen input and involvement. This can become tricky. On the one hand, it sounds like a clearly desired goal to have more people involved with the campaign, with more ideas flowing, with greater participation. On the other hand, it can be chaotic: following the whims and wishes of the moment instead of concentrating on a consistent, long-term strategy; listening to the loudest voices rather than the voices of those voters who could carry the candidate to victory; having a thousand messages, and no clear message at all; and, like

Howard Dean, being overtaken by the demands of supporters and losing control of the campaign.

Third, television will continue to be an important medium for campaign advertising. But, perhaps in the most fundamental transformation, communication has exploded into whole new ways of reaching voters. Free media, once confined to television, radio, or newspaper coverage, now find an unlimited home in YouTube and other web video sites. Likely voters are now reached through Internet advertising, RSS feeds, podcasts, interactive websites, social media platforms, blogs, microblogs (Twitter), text messages, and that old online standby, email.

Fourth, campaigns have speeded up dramatically. The campaign must expect to be engaged twenty-four hours a day. Polling results, field information, targeting and early voting data can all be received, analyzed and put into action in hours rather than days or weeks. The campaign now sleeps only when the election is over.

Fifth, guesswork, instinct and experience are still key, but they are supplemented by research, metrics, and advances in market research and data collection. It now becomes easier for a campaign to know if an ad campaign is working through focus group and dial meter research, by the

Table 1.1 Twentieth Century and Twenty-First Century Campaign Models

Twentieth Century Model	*Twenty-First Century Model*
Consultants dominate in creating strategy, in maintaining message discipline, in communicating with public, and getting voters out to vote on election day	Consultants dominate; online component becomes integral part of campaign
Top-down approach	More fluid, with ideas, direction, and support from grassroots
Television as most important communication medium	Television important, but explosion of new media, free media online
Relatively more time to craft messages, responses, and analysis	Campaign speeds up; running at 24/7 speed
Much of campaign based on guesswork, instinct, and past experience	Heavier reliance on research, data, metrics to guide the campaign
Fundraising through big ticket items; expensive direct mail solicitation; few small-amount donors	Big ticket fundraising important; small-amount donor opening up through inexpensive online technology
Except for presidential contests, limited involvement of citizens, beyond voting	Greater involvement of citizens, activists; sense that campaign is directly connected to them; well-financed outside forces.

click-through rates of online advertising, by the analysis of microtargeting information, and other techniques.

Sixth, campaigns still rely on big-dollar givers, but now can also have inexpensive access to small-amount donors, thanks to online contributing via email, texting, websites, and online advertising. The universe of money givers can be expanded many fold, using techniques often seen in public radio or other nonprofit fundraising schemes. At the same time, however, outside forces and interests have been given free hand to spend as much as they can raise to try to influence voters and affect election results.

Seventh, thanks to online communication, voters can have a greater sense of participation in a campaign. They can be mobilized, they can mobilize themselves, meet with likeminded activists, more easily contribute time, money, and energy to a campaign. Of all the aspects of the twenty-first century campaign model, this is the most promising for bringing about greater participation. However, outside interest groups, shadowy organizations with misleading names, and unreported campaign funds offer the real possibility that the entire election process will be funded and controlled by the super-rich.

The twenty-first century model recognizes the continuing need for consultants and campaign specialists, but it also recognizes that campaigns stuck in the old traditions and practices of the 1980s and 1990s are destined to be left behind and ultimately become non-competitive. And those campaigns which fail to appreciate and use the craft and techniques of the twentieth century model are likewise destined to become non-competitive.

2 Communicating with Voters

The New Media

San Francisco Mayor Gavin Newsom, 41, today took to the new media to formally announce he's running for governor—by directly addressing hundreds of thousands of supporters simultaneously via YouTube, Facebook and Twitter.

—San Francisco Chronicle (2009)

The virtual image is as mesmerizing as it is creepy. Meg Whitman, the leading Republican candidate for governor and the former chief executive of eBay, stands in front of a private jet, her lips peeled back from thick gums, and virtually snorts into the camera, "California, let me take you for a ride."

—New York Times (2010)

Senator Ted Cruz sent out this Tweet: "I'm running for President and I hope to earn your support."

—@TedCruz (March 23, 2015)

Neither the Gavin Newsom campaign announcement, the news item about the creepy Meg Whitman avatar, nor Ted Cruz's tweet would have made any sense to readers just a few years ago. In the 1990s, the term "new media" was just coming into our vocabulary. Blogging, social networking, RSS feeds, vlogs, Web 2.0, meetups, avatars, crowdsourcing, and tweets—all of these terms were unknown a decade ago. As late as the 2004 presidential election, new media did not include YouTube, which had not been invented yet, and Facebook and other social media sites, which were still in their infancy and centered around college campuses, not the wider commercial or political world (see Appendix B for a timeline of significant technology milestones in twenty-first century campaigning).

Just as online communication has profoundly changed the way we interact with one another, so too, have political campaigns made enormous changes in the way they communicate with people, the way people communicate with campaigns, and the way citizens, activists and voters communicate with one another about elections and campaigns. During the

Table 2.1 First Use of Selected Online Communication Tools in Political Campaigns

Websites	1992
Email	1992
Text messaging	2000
Blogging	2003
Social networking	2004
YouTube	2006
Twitter	2008

1990s, we first saw elected officials, candidates, political parties, and citizen activists using email and websites to communicate with others.[1] The Clinton campaign was the first to use the Internet in its 1992 presidential bid. Very few people in 1992, or for that matter throughout the 1990s, had access to computers or the Internet. Edward M. Kennedy (Democrat-Massachusetts) was the first U.S. senator to have a website. Created in May 1994, it was a rudimentary site, with a long, awkward URL address. Several months later e-democracy.org, a website to assist civic organizations in Minnesota, distributed information online then hosted the first online debates for gubernatorial and senatorial candidates in October 1994. The following year, the Democratic National Committee became the first major U.S. political party to host its own website. Then came Republican presidential nominee, Bob Dole, who announced his campaign's website address (albeit incorrectly) during the closing minutes of a presidential debate with President Bill Clinton in October 1996.

In these early days, there was excitement over the potential of online communication, and the prospect of campaigns being changed forever by email and the Internet, if candidates and organizations were savvy enough to harness their power. But for most observers, both scholars and practitioners, online communication for political campaigns then was still very much a work in progress.

Yet, in no other aspect of campaigning has there been so many profound changes. Political communications have been utterly transformed during the past decade, and campaign professionals have had to either change, adjust to new media, learn to use its potential—or to suffer the consequences of being uncompetitive.

What Has Changed in the Past Fifteen Years?

The Wired Nation

The Internet, email, cell phones, and mobile devices are now ubiquitous in American society. As of January 2014, a total of 87 percent of American adults (age eighteen and above) stated that they use the Internet, according to a survey by the Pew Research Center.[2] When Pew began tracking these figures in March 1995, just 12 percent of American adults were connected to the Internet, with that percentage climbing steadily over the years. By early 2014, an overwhelming 97 percent of young adults (age eighteen to twenty-nine) used the Internet. Still lagging, however, were those sixty-five and older (57 percent) and persons making less than $30,000 a year (77 percent). In mid-2011, 35 percent of American adults owned a smart phone, but by early 2015, that percentage had jumped to 64 percent. Again, young adults had the highest percentage of smart-phone users, at 85 percent. Text-messaging, photo-sharing, social media, and that old standby, email, were the most used features on smart phones.[3]

Where does the public get its information about political campaigns? Despite the inroads of online communication, in presidential contests television still dominates. For the 2008 presidential election, the Pew Research Center found in a January 2008 survey that adult Americans "regularly learn something" about the elections from local television news (40 percent), cable news networks (38 percent), nightly network news (32 percent), daily newspapers (31 percent), and the Internet (24 percent). Internet figures have grown through each of the most recent presidential election cycles. In the 2000 election, only 9 percent of the public said that it got its news from the Internet, and in 2004, just 13 percent.[4] However, there was a considerable gap between young adults and those over fifty: young adults, age eighteen to twenty-nine, get much less of their campaign news from television, radio, and newspapers than older people, and young adults get far more (42 percent) of their news from the Internet than older voters (15 percent). By the 2012 presidential election, television slid somewhat from its earlier spot, with more people, especially young adults, getting more of their news and information from mobile devices and other forms of online communication.[5]

Voters who are comfortable with and use online technologies, however, expect that politicians and political candidates will use these tools. In its fourth annual survey of voter expectations, released in October 2009, the e-Voter Institute found that voters are engaged in a "wider range of political activities online," that the Internet is becoming "increasingly integrated" into everyday lives and that the expectations that voters have for candidates and advocates "remained remarkably consistent during the last four years." Voters in the 2009 survey expected candidate campaigns to have an official website (85 percent), email (68 percent), television ads on their official website (66 percent); to conduct fundraising online (63 percent), and have online advertisements (60 percent), blogs and podcasts (57 percent). In just two categories, participating in social networking sites (49 percent) and Twitter (42 percent) did fewer than a majority of those surveyed expect campaigns to have these online tools.[6]

The Technology and Tools of Online Communication

As new online technologies have emerged, they have been incorporated into political campaigns, sometimes quickly, and other times, hesitantly and cautiously.

Campaign Websites

By 1996, campaign websites had been created for several presidential candidates, about half the U.S. Senate candidates, and about 15 percent of those running for seats in the House of Representatives. Most of the sites were just electronic versions of campaign brochures and literature.[7]

By the 2000 and 2002 campaigns, websites became common features. Some online activists and observers were talking about the profound changes that online communications would bring, changing forever the way campaigns are run. However, in their assessment of the place of the Internet in future elections, political scientists Bruce Bimber and Richard Davis took a sober look, and concluded that Internet campaigning helped to reinforce political attachments, to mobilize activists to contribute funds, to volunteer their time, and "just maybe—to vote." They recognized that the Internet was a niche communication tool, directed at highly specific audiences, that it would become highly effective to mobilize those who are politically active and interested, but predicted that the Internet would "not produce the mobilization of voters long predicted."[8]

Political scientists Stephen Schneider and Kristen Foot looked at the growth of campaign Internet site features from 2000 to 2004. They found that websites grouped features in four common areas: informing (with features presenting issues, campaign news, biography, speeches, photos and campaign ads); involving (online donations, volunteer, sign up for email, campaign calendar events, and campaign store); connecting (endorsements, links to government, civic and advocacy groups, political parties, and comparisons to other candidates); and mobilizing (sending links, e-paraphernalia, offline distribution of campaign materials, letters to the editor, action management sites or sections).[9] The authors found a slight increase from 2000 to 2004 in informing, a sharp increase in the practice of involving, a slight increase in the proportion of campaigns engaged in connecting, and mobilization was beginning to emerge in 2004.[10]

The innovations first came from the Dean campaign, with its connection with Meetup.com, the creation of the first presidential candidate blogsite, its own social network site, *Deanlink*, its personalized page for fundraising, *Deanspace*, and a virtual community for young people, *Generation Dean*. Several of the Dean online technology team alumni created Blue State Digital, an online technology firm, and later worked directly on the Obama campaign or as consultants to it.[11]

The primaries for the 2008 presidential race began to get interesting when Hillary Clinton introduced herself to the American public with an Internet video announcement: "I'm in it to win it" she announced from what looked like her well-lit living room, and she wanted to begin a dialog with the American people, "Let the conversation begin." The websites of the 2008 candidates were not revolutionary, but evolutionary, adding and refining the features already in place by 2004. Receiving the most attention, and most traffic, was the MyBarackObama (MyBO) segment of the Obama for America website. What was new in 2008 and expanded during the 2012 election was the enormous potential for posting campaign related videos on the newly created YouTube and the possibilities of social networking.

YouTube and Web Videos

During the 2004 presidential campaign, Internet audio and video files were added to the arsenal of communication tools. The most watched such web video file came from JibJab Media in July 2004. It featured cut-out cartoonlike figures of John Kerry and George Bush singing a political version of "This Land is Your Land." Once it was shown on television, viewers flocked to the JibJab site, and there were 65 million hits from throughout the world. Many other video and audio clips were added to the mix, from amateur videos, cartoons, parody sites, and clips from the campaigns themselves. We were now seeing the Wild West of campaign communication: some videos were tasteless, raunchy, factually untrue, and so provocative that they could not be shown on television.

Then came YouTube, the web video site created in 2005 by three early employees of PayPal. YouTube was not publicly launched until late 2005, but it immediately became enormously popular. By mid-2006, videos were being watched an estimated 100 million times a day on YouTube.[12] Then in October of that year, Google purchased the site for $1.65 billion. It didn't take long before candidates for public office started taking advantage of YouTube and other sites that offered free web video space.

In the 2008 presidential elections, YouTube hit its stride. It created YouChoose, space on YouTube where presidential contenders could post videos. Barack Obama made the most use of this vehicle, posting 1,839 videos with an astounding 132.8 million viewers; John McCain posted 329 videos with 26.3 million viewers. YouTube became a platform for candidates to bypass the established media and go directly to viewers online. Obama's explanation of why he changed his mind, deciding to forego public campaign financing for the general election, was posted on YouTube and viewed by more than 300,000 people during the first weeks, and more than 4 million viewers watched Obama's entire 37-minute speech on race relations in America.[13] The music video set to an Obama speech, "Yes, We Can" by hip-hop artist Will.i.am had over 10 million hits.

YouTube also joined up with CNN to produce two presidential debates, first in July 2007 among the Democratic contenders, and then in December for the Republican hopefuls. These were the first presidential debates that took questions posted online by viewers rather than having the questions posed by a panel from the mainstream media. Over 3,000 questions were posted online, and sixty-eight were asked of Democrats and thirty-one went to the Republican candidates.[14]

Another web video company offered services for candidates. UStream, created in 2007, is a website that allows live webcasting and video streaming of events online. Nearly all of the 2008 presidential candidates used UStream to allow voters to ask them questions. One Democratic long-shot candidate, former U.S. senator Mike Gravel (Democrat-Alaska) was the first to stream an alternate debate using UStream.[15] Adding its voice to the mix of video streaming sites was cable television network Comedy Central, which established Indecision2008, inviting viewers to download videos and read blogs from Stephen Colbert and Jon Stewart.

YouTube, UStream, and other web videos sites, along with social networking sites, discussed below, and videos embedded in emails provided quick, relatively inexpensive ways for candidates and causes to bypass the traditional media outlets and go directly to audiences online. There was no need to take a video clip and try to persuade a television station to show it, or a newspaper to comment upon it. Up it goes online for all to see.

Email, Cell Phones, and Twitter

One of the oldest technologies is still one of the most important: electronic mail. Presidential candidates in 1996 and congressional candidates in 1998 began using email as a vehicle for communicating with supporters. By the 2000 presidential contest, email had become a weapon of choice, and one of the central goals of campaigns using it was to connect email addresses with other demographics, such as voting history, home address, and other information.

At the time, email was indeed the killer application. Online communications expert Michael Cornfield observed in 2004 that email would outperform a website "ninety-nine days out of a hundred." Email is sent to a defined address, it is read, it is easier to respond to, and it is harder for the press and the political opposition to monitor than a website.[16] Over the years, campaigns have become more interactive: posting pictures, videos, links to other information, and frequently including "Donate Now" buttons. Emails could spiral out virally, as supporters would send the message to friends and associates.

One of the innovations in the 2000 presidential election came from the Gore campaign. Through emails to supporters and followers, it encouraged them to text message or email their own friends, to get them interested in Gore's campaign.[17] By the 2008 and 2012 presidential campaigns, text messaging and friend-to-friend encouragement were used on a massive scale.

Not until the mid-2000s did campaigns begin to understand the potential of cell phones as communication devices. Mobile phone communication had caught on in other parts of the world.[18] Over a million citizens in the Philippines were rallied to the streets, by using mobile text messaging, to protest against president Joseph Estrada in 2001. Hundreds of thousands of protestors were mobilized by text messaging demanding a rematch between Viktor Yuschenko and Prime Minister Viktor Yanukovych during Ukraine's "Orange Revolution" in 2004.

With the creation of the smart phone, particularly the RIM Blackberry, the Apple iPhone, the Nokia N900, and the Google Android, campaigns have been able to develop smart phone applications to help mobilize volunteers, facilitate fundraising, and other services. The Obama 2008 and 2012 campaigns were exceptionally good at using text messaging and smart phone applications. This is discussed in further detail as well as other aspects of smart phone technology in Chapter 7.

Twitter was created in early 2006 by Jack Dorsey as a way to send short messages (just 140 characters) to keep up with friends.[19] It went public in March of that year. Several 2008 presidential candidates, starting with John Edwards, Joe Biden, and Barack Obama used Twitter to communicate with followers. Since then, candidates have routinely added Twitter to their repertoire of online communication devices. The agility of online communication was demonstrated in the 2009 Virginia gubernatorial race. The *Washington Post* ran an exposé of Republican candidate Bob McDonnell's masters thesis, which many of his opponents considered anti-women. To counter this, McDonnell's campaign ran ads and posted on its blog site the favorable comments and support from women. The message also went out to thousands of Virginia supporters through email, Facebook postings, and Twitter.[20]

Simply tumbling out email or Twitter messages on a daily basis does no good, unless there is an authenticity and a relationship built between voters and the candidate. Joe Rospars, founding partner of Blue State Digital, cautioned that

> You can have Twitter and email but it doesn't necessarily mean you are doing things differently. There are political organizations whose strategy is to just use these new channels to play the same old game—to spin the press. You must use these channels to speak to people in a two-way conversation and really engage at a human level.[21]

Political and Campaign Blogs

Political blogs have fundamentally changed the way citizens interact with candidates and elections, even perhaps revolutionizing citizen participation.[22] Blogs can be started by anyone, with little or no editorial control, except perhaps self-policing; topics and discussions are wide open, and all who are interested can participate (see Further Reading for a partial listing of some of the more interesting political blogs).

The Institute for Politics, Democracy and the Internet (IPDI) of George Washington University conducted a survey of registered California voters in the summer of 2006 to determine who paid attention to political blogs.[23] IPDI found that the audience for political blogs as a news source concentrated on a few dozen blogs, rather than thousands. Daily blog readers, which constituted just 9 percent of the respondents, were disproportionately men, highly educated with a higher income than the general public, with a median age of 49, who placed themselves at the ends of the ideological/political spectrum, and were heavily involved in politics.

Blog sites were used to help raise campaign funds, fuel voter resentment, and encourage citizens of Connecticut to vote against two-term incumbent Democratic senator Joseph I. Lieberman in 2006. Lieberman had dismayed many Democrats who thought he was too comfortable with the policies of President George W. Bush, most personified in the senator's embrace of the Bush administration's Iraq war policies and a literal embrace, known as "The Kiss," when in January 2005, Bush kissed Lieberman on the cheek when the president was walking to the dais of the House of Representatives to deliver his State of the Union address.[24] The beneficiary of liberal Democratic ire was Ned Lamont, wealthy insurgent candidate who decided to challenge Lieberman for the Democratic nomination. Lamont was helped by liberal blogs that had national audiences, particularly DailyKOS, MyDD, FireDogLake.com, and MoveOn.org, as well as Connecticut- and locally based blog sites. Thanks in large measure to online fundraising and communication coming from blogsites, and because of his own personal wealth, Lamont pulled an upset victory over Lieberman. Yet, in the general election, Lieberman, who now ran as an Independent, was able to defeat Lamont and his Republican opponent. This insurgency campaign showed how potent online communication could be in channeling voter dissatisfaction, a lesson not lost on Tea Party activists in 2010 and subsequent elections.

The first presidential campaign blog was that of Howard Dean, created in 2003, then blogs were used extensively by John Kerry and George W. Bush in the 2004 general election.[25] Since that time, presidential and many other national and state candidates have used blogs to communicate with followers.

Social Networking

Beginning in 1995 with Classmates.com, social networks, such as Friendster, MySpace, and later Facebook became very popular. Social networks soon moved beyond high school and college students, to broader interests and as a political communication tool first appeared during the 2004 Democratic primaries, when Howard Dean's campaign used Meetup.com. Soon other campaigns both at the presidential and congressional level began to use social networking sites to identify new supporters, to energize their base, to help them communicate, host house parties and fundraise.[26]

Former senator and presidential candidate John Edwards signed up for more social networks than any other presidential candidate in 2008, a total of at least twenty-three sites. While Barack Obama generated more "friends" on his social network sites and on visits to YouTube, Edwards during the early days of the primaries had a more dynamic web presence: Flickr, MySpace, YouTube, Facebook, even Blip.tv and 43Things.com.[27]

In the end, the Obama campaign had a huge presence on social network sites. There were over 2.2 million supporters on the various Obama Facebook sites, 800,000 on MySpace, and substantial following on LinkedIn and other social network sites. The Obama campaign went right to the source: it recruited twenty-four-year-old Chris Hughes, co-founder of Facebook, to help develop the campaign's formidable and innovative online presence. More than 2 million persons logged on to MyBO (MyBarackObama), and through it were able to contribute funds, collect money from friends, develop communities and create support groups. Through MyBO there were 400,000 blog postings, 35,000 volunteers were recruited, and 200,000 off-line events were held. By election day, Obama had "friended" more than 7 million supporters.[28] As Jascha Franklin-Hodge, former Dean operative and co-founder of the digital consulting firm Blue State Digital put it, on every metric the Obama campaign "has operated on a scale that has exceeded what was done before."[29]

By the 2012 presidential campaign season, so much had changed in social media: Facebook had grown to over a billion users worldwide, Twitter grew to 500 million users, and other sites expanded in popularity. A full 82 percent of American adults received some of their news about the elections from social media.[30] Nearly any serious candidate for political office now has a social networking site. It is an inexpensive way to reach supporters, connect with like-minded people and solicit money. Start-up companies have also jumped into the business. Joining the ranks of Facebook, LinkedIn, and others in the social networking market are new social networking sites dedicated exclusively to campaigning and issue advocacy causes.

Online Advertising

Political advertising on Internet sites has been with us since 1998, when Peter Vallone, a candidate for governor in New York, posted online advertisements against his opponent, incumbent governor George Pataki.[31] The use of political advertising on the Internet, however, grew slowly. Looking at the 2004 presidential race and the 2008 presidential primaries, Michael Cornfield and journalist Kate Kaye argued that online advertising "remains in the prehistoric era" of development.[32] They noted that during the first eight months of 2004, the candidate campaigns, national parties, and major 527 organizations had spent about $2.66 million on banner ads. Yet this was less than 1 percent of the amount spent on television buys in the 100 largest markets during that period.

During the pre-primary year of 2007, the campaigns of Mitt Romney, John McCain, and Barack Obama ran almost all the online ads purchased by the candidates; Hillary Clinton, Mike Huckabee and the rest of the field of twenty ran just 1 percent of the online ads.[33] By the end of the election, the Obama campaign spent some $16 million on online media—a tiny fraction of the complete media buys. The largest portion of that online money, roughly $7.5 million went to Google AdWords. About $3.6 million was spent on online ads by the McCain campaign. Just $643,000 of Obama's online advertising went to Facebook.[34]

A new marketing theory, called Long-Tail Marketing, argues that businesses and political candidates can communicate better with those they are trying to reach by going to small, niche markets rather than relying on broadcasting to larger audiences. The 2008 U.S. Senate campaign of Minnesota Democrat Al Franken used long-tail techniques to reach voters. It targeted more than 125 niche groups, with more than 1,000 pieces of persuasive online advertising, for less than a $100,000 budget. "The trick," noted Josh Koster of Chong Design, "is to be everywhere, with tightly targeted messages." For example, when a Minnesota farmer looked on the search engine Google, the campaign had bought keywords, hundreds of them, like "farm supply," "feed stores," or "large animal veterinarian." When the farmer entered those words in his search, up would pop an appropriate Franken ad.[35]

The Republicans were not long to learn the lesson of online communication. Six months before the 2010 mid-term elections, Republican House candidates were outspending their Democratic counterparts on online advertising by a three-to-one ratio.[36] While Google was dominant in capturing online advertising revenues in 2008, Facebook was catching up to it in 2010. Andrew Bleeker, director of new media at AKPD, the Democratic consulting firm best known as the home of David Axelrod and David Plouffe, noted that the audiences for Facebook and Google are different. Google's search ad targeting is keyed to selected words—for example, "environmentally friendly" or "fiscal integrity"—whereas Facebook is aimed at different audiences—for example, friends of Barack Obama or Michigan Democrats.[37]

During the 2012 presidential campaign, online advertising really came into its own, with the Romney and Obama campaigns spending seven times more on online ads than in 2008.[38] The online advertising was a mix of videos embedded in banner ads, email, mobile phone ads, traditional video ads, and online radio sources like Pandora. The Obama online campaign invested more heavily than the Romney campaign, claiming 93.3 percent of the online market share during the general election. Online communications expert Julie Germany summed up the 2012 campaign by noting that the "Obama campaign gained far more visibility and incorporated more nuanced and sophisticated messaging to accompany their targeting efforts."[39]

How the Nature of Campaigns Has Changed Over This Time

With the introduction of these online communication tools, political campaigns have undergone some important transformations, with some results being quite positive, and others not so.

Nearly thirty years ago, before email, the Internet and the online revolution, political scientists Jeffrey Abramson, F. Christopher Arterton, and Gary Orren identified six properties that distinguished new communication technology from the old. The newer technologies 1) greatly increased the volume of information; 2) allowed for instant communication in "real time" and without regard to space; 3) increased the viewer's control of what will be received and when it will be received; 4) increased the sender's control of who receives the message; 5) decentralized control over the mass media; and finally, 6) allowed for much greater two-way communication.[40] The authors were primarily talking about the advent of satellites, cable television, bulky cell phones, videocassette recorders, facsimile machines, and the first generation of personal computers.[41] But their observations also make sense today. Writing in 2014, online communications expert Alan Rosenblatt observed that digital campaigns are fundamentally different from traditional campaigns in four major ways: digitally networked campaigns are ubiqituous, unfiltered, powerful, and they are social. Rosenblatt sees the last feature, the social aspect, as the true power: "Each time someone shares a photo, video, or text message, it gets passed along from friend to friend, from trusted messenger to trusted messenger."[42]

Great Increase in the Volume of Information

Looking back at 1996, it seems almost light years away when thinking about online communication. Then came websites, email, blogs, social networking, video webs, smart phone applications, Twitter and the rest. The smartest presidential, congressional, and statewide campaigns began adopting all of these communication tools. So did their opponents; so too, their friends and allies. And, of course, so too did the old and new media. By the mid-2000s, the attentive public had an incredible, bewildering array of information available about presidential campaigns. For example, researchers from the Pew Research Center categorized 63 million "online news consumers" during the 2004 election.[43] The researchers found that these online consumers went to campaign websites, newspaper online sources, and other sites:

- 34 million researched the policy issues of candidates
- 31 million went online to see how candidates were doing in the polls
- 20 million researched candidate voting records
- 18 million participated in online polls
- 14 million got information on where to vote
- 4 million signed up to volunteer, help register votes, and get people out on Election Day.

Long ago, the campaign manager or campaign press secretary would nervously open up the newspapers, watch the evening news, and perhaps check the wire stories to see if the campaign was being attacked, or that some bad news was about to impact the campaign. Mike McCurry, former press secretary to President Bill Clinton reminisced about campaign communication: "We had a conference call every night to discuss how the networks' nightly newscasts portrayed the election." But then McCurry added, "That's utterly useless now."[44] McCurry was talking about his experience in the 2004 presidential election.

But in 2008 and beyond, it was just as useless to concentrate on the evening network news when so much else is part of the noise and rush of contemporary communication. What are they saying in the Huffington Post? What are yesterday's poll numbers posted on Polling.com showing? Did you see that Twitter posting from our opponent? Are we following that potentially damaging rant on RedState.com blog site? Did you see how much traffic that YouTube posting is getting? Are we getting any traction from our pop-up ads on Google? What are they doing on our opponent's Facebook page? Did you see the analysis in today's RealClear Politics.com posting? Are we following the podcasts from Instapundit?

Table 2.2 Online Metrics for the 2008 Presidential Campaign

	Obama	*McCain*
Facebook friends on Election Day	2,397,253	622,860
Unique visits to campaign websites on week ending Nov. 1	4,851,069	1,464,544
Online videos mentioning candidate	104,454	64,092
Campaign-made videos posted on YouTube	1,822	330
Total hours people spent watching campaign videos (as of October 23)	14,600,000	488,000
Cost of equivalent purchase of 30-second TV ads	$46.9 million	$1.5 million
References to campaign's voters contact operation on Google	479,000	325

Source: Andrew Rasiej and Micah L. Sifry, "The Web: 2008's Winning Ticket," *Politico*, November 12, 2008.

The breakthrough in online communication was the 2008 presidential election. Andrew Rasiej and Micah L. Sifry, founder and editor respectively of the Personal Democracy Forum, tallied the online metrics for that campaign. Table 2.2 shows some of their findings.[45]

According to divinity Metrics, during the last 400 days of the 2008 presidential campaign, 104,545 videos about Obama (made by the campaign and by amateurs) were uploaded, and were viewed about 889 million times. There were 64,092 such videos about McCain, which were viewed about 554 million times.[46]

Instant Communication

As seen in Chapter 3, the political campaign has definitely speeded up over the past two decades. Long gone are the days when the only electronic news was the fifteen-minute and thirty-minute television newscast, appearing in the morning, noon, 6:00 p.m. and 11:00 p.m. time slots. With the proliferation of the 24/7 news cycle came 24/7 politicking. Experience had shown that when an opponent attacked, one's campaign would have to attack back with equal ferocity as soon as possible, to blunt or negate the charges against your candidate. Campaigns developed immediate response mechanisms, with the media team ready to fire back with video clips and soundbites.

With online communication, campaigns run at warp speed. A campaign can be hit with critical information at all times of the day or night, and in the pin-ball like atmosphere of a heated contest, particularly in its final days, bad news can come with the speed of digital communication. It could be a blog posting, an email charge gone viral, a nasty video posted on YouTube, a Twitter feed, or any one of a variety of online sources.

Why Wait for the Facts? Let the Comments Fly

In the late 1990s, the Drudge Report, a portal website for politics, was just getting started, and saw its breakthrough during the Monica Lewinsky/Bill Clinton soap opera. As website designs go, it was a rudimentary site serving chiefly as a portal linked to news sources, commentators, and other media sites. The Drudge Report became a newsworthy and somewhat unique site because it became an incubator for rumor mongering. A hot tip comes in, and immediately it is posted on the website. Is it true? Has it been confirmed? It apparently doesn't matter; the rumor gets posted and millions of viewers can judge for themselves. Such practices, of course, violate the ethics and norms of professional journalism. But with Drudge, and later for some of the hundreds of blogsites devoted to politics and opinion, checking facts no longer was the standard of caution. The Drudge Report continues to have heavy traffic, logging in million of viewers a day. By July 1, 2015, the Drudge Report claimed 28.8 million viewers that day and 8.8 billion viewers during the past 365 days.[47]

Rumors during the 2008 presidential contest were bountiful. Whisper and rumor campaigns have always been part of political campaigns, but the online nature took them to a different, more sinister level. Psychology professor Nicholas DiFonzo, who had been studying political rumor-mongering for twenty years, observed that he had never seen so many rumors as seen in 2008.[48] The rumors appeared to focus on the two least known of the contenders for office. Soon after Sarah Palin stepped onto the national stage, the false rumors started flying: she was part of a group of far-right Alaskans who wanted to secede from the Union; she tried to ban Harry Potter books from the Wasilla, Alaska, library; she advocated teaching creationism in the high schools of her state; she was Trig's grandmother (not his mother).[49]

The most vicious and ugly rumors were directed against Barack Obama: he was a Muslim; he wasn't born in America; he was a socialist; he was endorsed by the Black Panthers; he made fun of the Bible; he didn't get into Harvard Law School on his own merits; he was responsible for the economic meltdown; his radical pal William Ayers ghost-wrote Obama's autobiography; Michelle Obama ordered caviar and room service at a hotel. None of these rumors happened to be true, but they were nevertheless being spread virally across cyberspace. The Obama campaign tried to quash rumors, even hosted a website called Fight the Smears, which corrected the falsehood, asked viewers to report viral smear campaigns, and named names of those responsible for the tactics.[50]

This kind of smear campaign can be launched against any candidate at any time, aided and abetted by easy and unfiltered online access. For those campaigns, like Obama's, that are capable of fighting back with instant online communications, anti-smear website presence, the malicious attacks become a nuisance. For others, who cannot or will not fight back, rumor and innuendo, spread anonymously over various online communication platforms, can critically damage their campaigns.

Is the Internet the culprit in this high level of rumor mongering? Former law professor and later Obama administration official Cass R. Sunstein argues that increasingly people are getting their information not from the major news channels, like the network television stations, but from online sites. They subscribe to email listservs or RSS feeds for their favorite sites. If they tend to be progressive or liberal, they go to Huffington Post or AlterNet to find stories that support their underlying beliefs; if they are conservative, they might gravitate to the Drudge Report or NewsMax.[51]

A study of political blogs during the 2004 election revealed, not surprisingly, that liberal blogs tended to link to other liberal blogs, and conservative blogs linked to other conservative blogs, but more frequently and in a denser pattern than liberal blogs.[52] Sunstein argues that the Internet "serves, for many, as a breeding group for extremism, precisely because like-minded people are deliberating with greater ease and frequency with one another." This is the process, he writes, of "cyberpolarization."[53] In many cases online communications are anonymous, postings in many cases are not filtered, and the minimum rules of decency and probity are thrown out the window.

The Ever-Present Camera and the Viral Response

Today, no candidate is safe from the prying eye of the television camera, the handheld camera, or the cell phone camera. A gaffe, an errant word or gesture, can be immediately captured by a campaign volunteer or by anyone holding a cell phone. Hillary Clinton was caught singing the national anthem horribly off-key at a campaign stop; John Edwards was caught primping for two full minutes in a television station's green room, meticulously combing his hair before an appearance. The subsequent YouTube video of Edwards combing his locks was set to Julie Andrews singing "I Feel Pretty" from *West Side Story*.

Journalists Chris Cillizza and Dan Balz mark the 2006 mid-term election as one that changed the rules of the game. This was the year of the "rogue videographers." In one example, future presidential candidate Mitt Romney's communication staff was alerted to a video bouncing around the Internet of comments Romney had made in 1994 about gays and abortion rights. Romney had since disavowed those statements. His team struck back within eight hours with a video of Romney rebutting the charges, and sending the video to supporters and friendly bloggers to ward off further damage.[54]

But the most politically consequential remark caught on video was the "macaca" moment for Senator George Allen, a Virginia Republican, running for re-election in 2006. Allen, widely viewed as a potential Republican candidate for president in 2008, was campaigning in rural western Virginia. He was being shadowed by a college student, who was a staffer for his rival's campaign. The student, an American citizen of Indian heritage, using a digital recorder captured Allen's speech before a friendly crowd. Allen turned toward the student, saying "This fellow here, over here with the yellow shirt, macaca, or whatever his name is. He's with my opponent. He's following us around everywhere. Let's give a welcome to macaca, here. Welcome to America and the real world of Virginia."[55]

That comment, recorded, and soon displayed on YouTube was picked up by media outlets worldwide and helped doom the senatorial (and once-promising presidential) ambitions of George Allen. Virginia, long a conservative, fairly homogeneous political culture, in recent years had been transformed, especially in the populous northern Virginia suburbs of Washington, D.C., into a polyglot of languages, cultures, and aspirations, no longer fixated on the commonwealth's civil war legacy. Allen's opponents were quick to point out that in earlier times, he kept a Confederate flag in his home, wore a Confederate flag in his lapel, and touted Confederate History Month—all symbols highly offensive to African Americans and other Virginians. "Macaca," a term rarely heard in America, nonetheless deeply offended members of the Washington chapter of the Association of Indians in America and many others. Allen should have won re-election handily, but lost by just a few thousand votes to James H. Webb, a former Republican and vocal anti-war critic. Not only did Allen's loss doom his presidential ambitions but his was one of six critical seats that Democrats captured, allowing them to reclaim majority status in the U.S. Senate. A demeaning and completely unnecessary remark, caught on digital recorder, uploaded to cyberspace, crashed a long-standing political career and brought Democrats to power.

Candidates now have no immunity from the prying, ever-present electronic eye. There is no room for looking bored, dozing off to sleep, singing off-key, or saying something inappropriate. A well-worn campaign trick is to provoke a candidate into saying something he or she would later regret, or to photograph a candidate in an awkward moment. That tactic is now magnified by campaign provocateurs, armed with cell phone cameras, ready to catch an opponent off-guard, willing to provoke a candidate into anger or worse: all the better to humiliate an opponent while posting such theatrics on a video website.

A lot of people on the Net have given up on traditional politics precisely because it was about television and the ballot box, and they had no way to shout back. What we've given people is a way to shout back, and we listen—they don't even have to shout anymore.

(Howard Dean 2003)[56]

Bottom Up and Open-Sourced

Veteran Democratic pollster Peter Hart summed up the impact of technology on the 2008 presidential campaign: "This is a big transformation in how campaigns operate, and it boils down to the power of one, the feeling that one individual can make a difference."[57] Successful, professional campaigns have always been driven from the top, down. Campaign consultants call the shots, develop the strategy, the message, and try to control the pace of the campaign. But now with the enormous opportunities and challenges of online communication, a new model is appearing, with citizen input encouraged and fostered.

This is probably the most important aspect of new media and online communication in election politics: in the best of campaigns (and the best of candidates), activists and even casual voters can feel a sense of sharing and participation. Through online communication, they share their ideas with the candidates, are encouraged to volunteer, meet and talk with others, share their experiences, and take some measure of ownership in the campaign. Campaigns, especially for the presidency, are far more than about the individual candidates: they are about understanding, sharing, and working together. Some of the most compelling questions in a campaign are these: Does the candidate understand my problems? Am I comfortable with him or her? Does the candidate share my values and convictions? That's what we saw particularly in the 2008 presidential campaign, with strong emotive force behind Barack Obama, and an even stronger force behind Sarah Palin on the Republican side.

Online communication can help strengthen and facilitate those bonds. We might say that the twenty-first century campaigning really began with Howard Dean and his reliance on grassroots activism. Yet that campaign failed. As political scientist Matthew R. Kerbel summed up, Dean's effort

> came to be defined by, and ultimately held hostage to, its grassroots component because of his inability to build a durable infrastructure, leaving the campaign ill-equipped to manage the everyday demands of traditional campaigning in an age still dominated by television.[58]

Barack Obama's campaign learned from Dean's mistakes. Top-down control is critical, never losing control to the enthusiasm of grassroots followers, but encouraging them to expand his campaign's reach, through more campaign funds, more volunteers, more energy and ultimately more votes. As Dean's campaign manager Joe Trippi observed, Obama maintained "command and control at the top while empowering the bottom to make a difference."[59]

Obama's campaign was able to convert the enthusiasm of his supporters in ways that McCain in 2000 and Dean in 2003 could not. As digital communications expert Monte Lutz noted, McCain failed to convert his 2000 online donors into votes and Dean in 2003 failed to convert the enthusiasm of his followers into effective victory in the Iowa caucus. But Obama did both. "The Obama campaign combined the embrace of online enthusiasm of Dean '04 with the discipline, organization, and hyper-targeting of the Bush re-election campaign."[60]

In summing up the online communication of the presidential candidates in 2008, Julie Germany observed that what was most revolutionary was the action of voters and supporters "who engaged in the election online, who conversed and interacted with each other, changed campaign history."[61]

Nearly all of the previous examples come from presidential elections during the first decade of the twenty-first century. The tools of online communication are now available to all, and even the smallest budget local campaign can take advantage of some of the aspects. However, political scientist Chapman Rackman has argued that it takes a cycle or two before congressional candidates adapt the technologies found in presidential races, and that state level candidates lag further behind. Writing in 2004, Rackman noted that "state legislative races are operating at a campaign level roughly comparable to those of presidential candidates of 1996."[62]

All the bells and whistles of online communication were readily available to each of the presidential candidates in 2008 and 2012, and to the twenty-two Republican and Democratic candidates in the 2016 presidential primaries, and the thousands of candidates for other offices from 2010 through 2016. The tools—email, social networking, RSS feeds, text messaging, and the like—are simply that, tools. Candidates without charisma, without excitement, without a compelling message, and above all, without authenticity cannot be lifted above the fray even with the slickest, fanciest online tool.

3   Communicating with Voters

The Old Media

The more [you] spend, the less it works. The less it works, the more [you] spend.

—Seth Godin on television advertising (1999)

It is truly extraordinary how far political media have come in the past twenty-five years. From the "stone age" of taking weeks to shoot and produce spots to the modern "tech age" of high-quality digital video; from time-consuming editing to instant changes with computer wizardry; from mere guesswork to a growing body of research about our audiences, focus groups, testing and audience targeting.

—Peter Fenn (2008)

Historically, close to two-thirds of all political advertising is compressed into the final sixty days of an election. This turns the battleground states into echo chambers from wall-to-wall political ads on television, radio, billboards and the Internet, to say nothing about incessant telephone calls.

—Evan Tracey (2013)

The overarching question for candidates and their campaign staffs is how they can wade through the clutter of offline and online communication to reach the right people, with the right message, at the right time, at an affordable price. For much of the second half of the twentieth century, candidates turned to television. Beginning with the early television commercials created by Madison Avenue agencies in 1952 for presidential candidates Dwight Eisenhower and Adlai Stevenson, television soon became the dominant means of communication for candidates for high office.[1] Radio and newspapers played important roles for political advertising, while newspapers and nightly local and national television newscasts were the main vehicles for informing the public about campaigns and elections. Direct mail marketing and telephone calls also became important tools of communication for candidates, particularly for those many candidates who could not afford expensive television advertising.

With so much attention focused on the new media, what has happened to the tried and true communication tools of the late twentieth century? Much has changed, but they still are dominant voices in political communication.

What Has Changed in the Past Fifteen Years?

Americans Still Watch a Lot of Television

Americans were watching more television in 2010 than ever before. As we get more connected and wired online, television is still the great universal medium. As a 2010 study for the Television Bureau of Advertising concluded: "by every measure, television reaches more consumers every day than newspapers, magazines, radio, the Internet and mobile media, and ... more time is spent with television."[2] Television, the report noted, reached 90 percent of American adults, who watch over five hours a day on average (much higher than any other medium); it is the primary source of local news, and by significant margins television advertising is seen as the most exciting, influential, persuasive, authoritative and engaging format.

The Nielsen Company, which tracks the viewing habits of Americans, reached similar findings, noting that the amount of time people spent watching television has been increasing. Each week in the first quarter of 2010, the average American watched roughly thirty-five hours of television and two hours of timeshifted TV through a digital video recorder (DVR), devices like TiVo which are now found in 35 percent of American homes. "It seems that, for the foreseeable future at least, America's love affair with the TV will continue unabashed," observed Matt Brady of the Nielsen Company. That love affair has continued, but as of mid-2015, there has been a gradual and steady decline in television viewing. Yet, some of that decline comes from viewers watching television shows on their computer screens, tablets and smartphones.[3]

Further Fragmentation of Audience

Long ago, the three networks—ABC, NBC, and CBS—dominated television. Then came cable television in the 1970s, and with it a whole host of niche television stations. Depending on one's wallet and desires, the television viewer may now have hundreds of stations available to watch at any one time. Further, as television has converted to digital format, there has been even further explosion in the number of television channels now available. The cable stations offer a wide range of choices, often going after niche markets: the Food Channel, Comedy Central, Cartoon Channel, Metro Chinese Language, movie, pay-per-view, religious, redneck reality TV, and sports channels, catering to all kinds of tastes. In January 2015, nearly three-fourths (72 percent) of U.S. households had high-definition television (HDTV), up dramatically from 2008, and viewers spent an average of three hours and forty-one minutes each month simultaneously watching TV and using the Internet.[4] More channels, more options, and fewer eyes on any one single source.

Television has also migrated to the Internet. For example, in March 2009, Jeff Bewkes, the chief executive officer of Time Warner, announced a plan to put all of its cable programming on the Internet, on places like Yahoo TV, MySpace, Hulu, and even YouTube.[5] Since then, other television networks have gone online, creating their own apps, and joining streaming services from Amazon, Netflix, Apple TV, and others.

There has also been a significant increase in the number of radio stations available. At the end of 2014, there were 15,432 radio stations, up from 12,000 in 1997.[6] Included in the mix are satellite radio stations. The satellite radio network XM developed POTUS (Politics of the United States), a special channel dedicated to covering the 2008 presidential election. It had more than 8.2 million listeners.[7] The number of high-definition (HD) radio stations has surpassed 1,900 and is growing.

By contrast, newspaper circulation is down. Newspaper circulation dipped precipitously in recent years, but rebounded somewhat during the presidential year of 2012. Since then, however, there has been a 3 percent annual erosion in circulation.[8] While online versions of newspapers, accompanying blogs, and online features bring more people to newspaper content, traditional news print doesn't have the same appeal.

Audience fragmentation presents both challenges and opportunities for political media consultants. The challenge, of course, is that instead of having to focus a message on three or four televisions stations, perhaps the local newspaper, and several radio stations, political campaigns and media buyers face this greatly fragmented audience. Audience fragmentation, observes veteran media consultant Peter Fenn, "has made it vastly more difficult to get our messages out to the people we want in sufficient enough numbers to really make an impact."[9] The opportunity lies in the niche marketing of many cable channels. If you want to reach young men, try ESPN, the Outdoor channel or Comedy Central; a LGBT audience, try Logo; conservative religious audience, try any one of a number of such channels. Redneck reality TV is your thing? There are plenty of choices on cable. Like radio, cable television offers far clearer narrrow-casted, defined audiences than network television.

Blocking Out Television Ads

What do audience members do when commercials are shown on their favorite television shows? According to the American Academy of

Advertising, many are not paying attention: 6 percent simply ignore the commercial, 14 percent say they mute the channel; 19 percent change channels; and 53 percent pay attention to something else while the commercial is running.[10]

Added to this, is the rapid growth of digital video recorders. "We are in a period of chaos," declared WNYC's Bob Garfield, in 2007. He was referring to the fragmenting of the old model of television advertising, with the rise of the Internet and the new media. He was also referring to the growing use of DVRs (digital video recorders), like TiVo, which can be set to record favorite television shows, and skip the commercials. DVRs were in just 2 percent of households in 2002, but were projected to be in nearly half by the end of 2010.[11] In a 2010 survey of 20,000 TiVo users, a full 66 percent skipped commercials during prime time network television time and for all television (cable and network), about 50 percent of ads were skipped. Adults fifty and older tended to be more patient with political ads: they viewed them 15 percent more than did other viewers who had digital video recorders.[12] Nielsen Company research for the first quarter of 2010 showed similar results. On the average, Americans spend nine hours and thirty-six minutes watching time shifted television per month, which is nearly a 15 percent increase from the first quarter in 2009.[13]

Compounding the problem for political advertising is the fact that viewers can now watch many of their favorite television shows through Hulu or other Internet sites, where the commercials (except for short Hulu sponsorship commercials) are deleted.

Still campaign advertising flows to television, and especially local television, because that is what people watch and where they turn to get their political news. In a June 2013 survey, Gallup found that 55 percent of respondents got their political information from television; 21 percent from the Internet; 9 percent from newspapers; 6 percent from radio; while 2 percent relied on word of mouth for their information.[14]

Increases in Presidential-Year Television Advertising, but in Selected Markets

During the 2004 election, there were more television campaign commercials than ever before. Counting all 210 media markets in the United States, and going up and down the electoral ladder, from presidential to local race, there were more than 3 million political spots. Altogether, the presidential candidates, the political parties and their allies broadcast more than 1 million ads in 2004, more than twice the number in 2000.[15] Yet, most Americans in 2004 barely saw any presidential political commercials.

The political ads were concentrated heavily in the battleground states, like Florida, Ohio, Pennsylvania, Iowa, and New Jersey, but in states that

Table 3.1 Television Spending For Candidates, Issue Policy, and Ballot Measures, 2008 Cycle

Candidates	$1,216,886,177
Issue policy	$354,532,070
Ballot measures	$267,918,430

Source: Campaign Media Analysis Group; reprinted in TVB.org Political Databank, "2008 Political Spending Overview." Available at http://www.tvb.org/arc/political databank/PDB_Spending_Overview.asp; accessed June 23, 2010.

were uncompetitive, like Texas, New York, California, and others, there were very few commercials.[16]

In 2008, the number of television commercials topped the 2004 totals. It was a record-breaking year for television advertising for elections and campaigns. Altogether, $1.83 billion was spent on television, with 66 percent of that being spent by candidates.

There were some national television buys from the presidential campaigns, notably during the Beijing Olympics and Obama's late October half-hour infomercial. But the lion's share of television ads went to local television stations; candidates spent 82 percent of their television ad buying on local television stations. Local cable came in a distant second (14.2 percent), followed by network television (2.4 percent) and national cable (1.4 percent).

Furthermore, television advertising was concentrated in key battle-ground states in 2008. Over 87 percent of the money spent after the party conventions went to television stations in eleven battleground states. The largest amount was spent in Florida ($42.2 million), Pennsylvania ($41.3 million), Ohio ($31.9 million), and Virginia ($27.2 million), with between $10 and $15 million spent in Wisconsin, Colorado, North Carolina, Michigan, Missouri, Indiana, and Nevada.[17] But these numbers paled by comparison to the television money spent during the 2012 general election in battleground states. Again the largest concentration of money went to Florida, but in 2012 it was $173 million. Next came Virginia ($151 million); then Ohio ($150 million); North Carolina ($97 million); Colorado ($73 million); and Iowa ($57 million).[17]

Table 3.2 Television Spending Patterns by Presidential Candidates, 2008

Local TV stations	$1.163 million	82.1%
Local cable	$200 million	14.2%
Network TV	$34 million	2.4%
National cable	$19 million	1.4%

Source: Campaign Media Analysis Group; reprinted in TVB.org Political Databank, "2008 Political Spending Overview." Available at http://www.tvb.org/arc/political databank/PDB_Spending_Overview.asp; accessed June 23, 2010.

This continues a trend found in the twentieth century. In the 1992 general election, both Ross Perot and George H. W. Bush spent most of their advertising budget on national buys, while Bill Clinton chose to target eighteen states for his ads. In 1996, Bob Dole's late general election ad buys concentrated on fourteen states. In 2000, there was hardly any money that went to national television ads, but instead went to target battleground states. Since then, political campaigns and outside expenditures have concentrated their media buying power on just a handful of battleground states, leaving uncompetitive states with very few television ads about the presidential election.[18]

Inventive Uses of Free Television

Commercial advertisers have to come up with inventive ways to get viewers' attention, other than simply launching another round of expensive commercials. Many have tried product placement (paying a hefty fee so that the can of soda drunk by the television characters is your product only). Political candidates can't do this, but they have been appearing more frequently on late-night talk shows or at the coin toss of a high-profile football game. Such appearances are usually confined to presidential candidates, not the average candidate for county sheriff.

Former Arkansas governor Mike Huckabee, running for the Republican nomination for president in 2008, was short of cash and desperate to get his message across. He took advantage of free local television, and gave nearly twenty television interviews every morning for four months prior to the first caucus in Iowa. He would go on everything from the conservative religiously oriented *700 Club*, to CNN, to *The Colbert Report*. "We estimate that was $200 million in free media," said his communications chief, Kirsten Fedewa. "The media was his base."[19] In 2016, Huckabee ran again for the Republican nomination, but with many more candidates, and particularly with Donald Trump dominating much of the news, it was difficult for Huckabee to reach the free media market.

Sitting presidents and candidates for office have not been reluctant to go on late night comedy shows during the late twentieth century. Presidential candidate Richard M. Nixon appeared taped on a five-second tape for Rowan & Martin's *Laugh-In*, in 1968, saying "sock it to *me*?" Eight years later, President Gerald Ford (during the 1976 campaign) videotaped the well-known *Saturday Night Live* opening: "Live from New York, It's Saturday Night!" Candidate Bill Clinton put on a pair of sunglasses and wailed his saxophone on the *Arsenio Hall Show* in 1992. During the 2000s, presidential candidates had frequently made their way to the guest chairs at *The Tonight Show* with Jay Leno (NBC), *The Late Show with David Letterman* (CBS), and *The Daily Show with Jon Stewart* (Comedy Central). The reason is simple: between 4 and 6 million viewers on the Leno and Letterman shows and 1.6 million primarily younger viewers on the Stewart show.

During the 2008 presidential election, candidates branched out to popular daytime television shows as well, like *Oprah*, *The Ellen DeGeneres Show*, *The Tyra Banks Show*, *Live with Regis and Kelly*, and *The View*.[20] Undoubtedly the most important appearance was that of Barack and Michelle Obama on the *Oprah Winfrey Show* in October 2006. Two economists from the University of Maryland estimated that Winfrey's enthusiastic endorsement of Obama (first uttered three weeks earlier on a *Larry King Live* interview) was worth 1 million votes in the Democratic primaries.[21] MTV and its "Choose or Lose" campaign teamed up with the social networking site MySpace.com to present the MTV Myspace Candidate Dialogue, which featured video clips of several presidential contestants fielding questions from young voters.[22]

In 2015, no one could touch the free media attention that was given to Donald Trump, the loud-mouthed, bombastic business and media entrepreneur who was running for the Republican presidential nomination. Trump sucked up nearly all the attention with his boasts, put-downs, and "tell it like it is" pronouncements. Texas senator Ted Cruz, New Jersey governor Chris Christie, and perhaps Kentucky senator Rand Paul were supposed to fill the role of anti-establishment truth-tellers, but they have been pushed out of the media spotlight by Trump, who during the pre-primary stage saw his popularity soar among disgruntled Republicans.

Increase in Negative Advertising

At the third presidental debate, held at Hofstra University, Hempstead, New York, on October 15, 2008, there was a heated exchange about McCain's television advertising:

OBAMA: And 100 percent, John, of your ads—100 percent of them have been negative.
MCCAIN: That's not true.
OBAMA: It absolutely is true.

Not quite. The *St. Petersburg Times* website PolitiFact.com notes that Obama was "cherry picking" his dates, probably relying on a report from the Wisconsin Advertising Project that noted that "nearly all" of McCain's ads from September 18 through October 4 were negative. Overall, the Wisconsin research showed that McCain's ads were 71 percent negative (certainly not 100 percent) and that Obama's were 61 percent negative.[23] Communications professor William Benoit noted that the 2008 television ads were the most negative in history. According to his analysis, the Obama ads were negative 68 percent of the time, compared to 62 percent of the time for McCain.[24] By contrast in 2004, the Bush ads were negative 64 percent of the time and the Kerry ads were negative 34 percent of the time. In another assessment, however, political scientist Darrell West saw a greater percentage of negative ads come in the 1984 and 1988 presidential elections than in the more recent campaigns.[25]

In other 2008 campaigns, candidates spent millions to introduce themselves to their audiences, contrast their record or their aspirations against those of their opponents, and in some cases attack the character of their opponents. Representative David R. Price (Democrat-North Carolina) introduced the "stand by your ad" provision, modeled after North Carolina law, into the Bipartisan Campaign Reform Act (BCRA) in 2002. All federal candidates now must acknowledge ownership of their television ads. Ironically, one of the most egregious ads came from the hotly-contested U.S. Senate campaign in North Carolina, between incumbent Elizabeth Dole and challenger, and ultimate winner, Kay Hagan.

ELIZABETH DOLE: I'm Elizabeth Dole and I approve this message.
NARRATOR: A leader of the Godless Americans PAC recently held a secret fund-raiser in Kay Hagan's honor.
ELLEN JOHNSON,   executive director of the Godless Americans PAC, but not identified as such in the commercial: There is no God to rely on.
JOHNSON: There was no Jesus.
[The ad then shows Bill O'Reilly, of the television show "The O'Reilly Factor" asking the Godless Americans PAC director, David Silverman the following]
O'REILLY: Taking "under God" out of the Pledge of Allegiance, you're down with that?
SILVERMAN [UNIDENTIFIED]:   We're down with that.
O'REILLY: "In God we trust"—are you going to whip that off the money?
SILVERMAN [UNIDENTIFIED]:   Yeah, we would.
NARRATOR: Godless Americans and Kay Hagan. She hid from cameras. Took Godless money. What did Hagan promise in return?
[The ad then shows an image of Hagan, with a female voice-over declaring: "There is no God!"]

The problem was that Kay Hagan, former Sunday School teacher, long-time member of the Presbyterian church, never said "There is no God," and the fund-raiser was not hosted by the Godless America PAC; it was just one of forty co-hosts of the event. Jody C. Baumgartner and his colleagues note that this ad, along with hard-hitting ones by Hagan, remained controversial through the end of the campaign, and was able to fit into the larger theme that Dole was "out of touch with North Carolinians and outside of the ideological mainstream of America."[26]

There is no evidence that requiring candidates to acknowledge ownership of the words and pictures launched against opponents will either temper or constrain them, but it does put them squarely on record.

After the U.S. Supreme Court ruled in *Citizens United v. Federal Election Commission* (see below) that corporations could spend unlimited amounts of funds on advocacy ads, Democratic members of the House of Representatives tried to put a "stand by your ad" requirement for corporate and other special interest ads. The bill, known as the Disclose Act, passed the House 219–206 in June 2010, banned spending on political campaigns by corporations that had $10 million or more in federal government contracts and by American corporations controlled by foreign citizens. It also prohibited corporations from coordinating spending with candidates or political parties, and required their chief executives to appear in any advertisement paid for by their companies. As part of the bill, there were exemptions for some of the most powerful interests, notably the National Rifle Association, the Sierra Club, and other large nonprofits. The legislation, however, faced a tough battle in the Senate, and did not become law.[27]

Negative advertising continued strong in the 2012 presidential election. In a wrap up analysis of television advertising, the *Washington Post* concluded that of the $404 million spent by the Obama campaign and its allies on television, some 85 percent of the ads could be characterized as negative. For Romney and his allies, $492 million was spent and an estimated 91 percent of the ads were negative.[28]

During the hotly contested 2014 Senate and House races, negative advertising again was the norm, pounding away at the character, reputation, ideology and beliefs, or voting records of candidates. Political consultants are no fools: they urge their clients, the candidates, Super PACs, and others to "go negative" because it works. Solid, effective negative ads can drive home a message, and the results will be visible in overnight tracking polls. However, it becomes harder to determine which ad or which set of circumstances affects voters' overnight attitudes with such a clutter of information available and relentlessly confronting voters during the heat of a general election.

Branding and Framing

One of the most important aspects of a political party or candidate's image is their brand. Political scientist Jennifer Lees-Marshment argues that branding is "how a political organization or individual is perceived overall. It is broader than the product ... a brand offers something additional, which is more psychological and less tangible."[29] Social scientist Catherine Needham writes that successful brands act as simplifiers, they are unique and clearly differentiated from the competition, they give reassurance, they evoke a positive image, and they are credible and deliver on their promises.[30]

Under the leadership of Newt Gingrich and his colleagues in 1994, the "Contract with America" was a key element in branding the Republican Party as the party of small government, national security, fiscal discipline, and seeker of moral correctness. Barack Obama in his 2008 presidential campaign had a coherent brand, along with a highly successful logo, colors, and thematic consistency.

For others, it was more difficult to mount a consistent, positive brand. The Hillary Clinton presidential campaign in 2007 was grappling over what image she should portray. With near-100 percent name recognition (and one of the few people like Oprah or Cher who were known to all by their first names only), but with high negatives among the general public, the questions became: how to present her, as "tough as a man" or a more humanized picture, the softer side. Chief strategist Mark Penn advocated presenting Clinton as a strong commander-in-chief who had deep knowledge of policy issues (reminiscent of the 3:00 in the morning television ad); Mandy Grunwald, the senior media consultant, wanted to present a more humanized, more personable and likeable candidate. What first emerged, according to political scientists Regina G. Lawrence and Melody Rose, was a gender strategy based on a "complex mix of toughness and feminine appeal, with toughness in the lead and feminine solidarity playing a supporting role." Ultimately the masculine fighter narrative, advocated by Penn, was the image that won the day and was amplified throughout the campaign.[31]

Hillary Clinton, known to all, with high negative marks, but also a loyal dedicated following is the front-runner for the 2016 Democratic nomination. Thus far, through the pre-primary phase, she has kept low-keyed, focused, building her war chest and her network of ground support. She is reluctant to take media questions, preferring to meet with carefully-selected citizens in quiet settings. Her team of advisers, many old Obama campaign hands, knowing that she would be faced with a barrage of attacks on her character, on State Department emails, and Benghazi, were essentially keeping their powder dry during this time, letting Donald Trump, Ben Carson, and others steal most of the headlines and attention.

"Framing," writes cognitive scientist and linguist George Lakoff, "is about getting language that fits your worldview. It is not just language. The ideas are primary—and the language carries those ideas, evokes those ideas."[32] "Inheritance tax" becomes "death tax"; "global warming" becomes "climate change"; and "vouchers" become "scholarships." Republican pollster Frank I. Luntz was at the forefront of the practical application of framing to politics. His book title states his overall philosophy, "What matters is not what you say, but what people hear."[33]

President Bill Clinton belatedly learned to play the game: he used Republican language to describe his agenda: "welfare reform," or "the era of big government is over." Republicans groaned, but could do little to stop him. Bush likewise used euphemisms to mollify critics or to lull the complacent: "healthy forests," "Clear Skies Initiative," or "No Child Left Behind."

The Democratic Party in 2007 launched a multi-year polling project, to find the right themes and words to counter the Republican attacks on immigration policy. Democrats chose to embrace the language of the tough, but fair, father figure. What do you call the 12 million persons who unlawfully live in the U.S.? Call them "illegal immigrants," not "undocumented workers." Democrats are now supposed to stress that it is "unacceptable" to have 12 million people living illegally in the U.S. and the government must "require" them to register and "get right with the law." America's Voice, a pro-immigrant rights group worked with the Center for American Progress founder John Podesta to come up with the language. Psychologist and political consultant Drew Westen assisted, and a team of Democratic pollsters surveyed swing districts in 2006 and 2007. The most significant shift in Democratic language is the path to citizenship: "It comes back to this idea: We give permission; we set the terms; it's under our control; and if you meet those conditions, you are us, welcome to America," Westen said of the new frame.[34] Probably no pollsters or focus groups were ever consulted, however, when Donald Trump in May 2015 blurted out his commentary on immigrants, bringing "drugs, crime and rapists," into the United States, or his solution, building a wall and making the Mexican government pay for it.

Faux TV

A growing trend in campaign advertising is what might be called "faux TV." The candidate is interviewed by a reporter, asked questions, there are cut-away interviews with people on the street, with the familiar ending, "reporting live from Ocean City, this is" your friendly television reporter. Except it is all contrived: it is not a neutral, objective interview; the questions asked are soft, easy, often misleading questions, and the reactions from people on the street are either prompted by misleading introductions or carefully edited; and the "reporter" works for the candidate.

This is what former governor of Maryland Robert L. Ehrlich, Jr., was doing in his comeback 2010 bid for governor against the man who beat him four years earlier, Martin J. O'Malley. The reporter, Andy Barth, in fact had been a long-time news reporter in Baltimore, but now was Erhlich's press secretary. The flattering three-minute commercial, disguised as a television news interview, was posted on YouTube, Facebook, and other sites.

O'Malley wasn't the first candidate to use this tactic, and certainly won't be the last. In 2008, Senator Christopher J. Dodd (Democrat-Connecticut) launched DoddTV, an Internet site showing Dodd's campaign in action. Further, Republican operatives were exposed when they created false Internet sites, claiming to be neutral news sites but in fact were campaign oriented. Earlier, President George W. Bush's Health and Human Services Department produced a series of videos about changes in Medicare. The "reporters" in the segments were HHS employees, not objective outside reporters. The Government Accountability Office (GAO) determined that the Medicare ads violated federal law.[35]

Citizens United Decision

In January 2010, the U.S. Supreme Court handed down a much anticipated decision that reshaped the constitutional protections of free speech and ruled unconstitutional parts of the Bipartisan Campaign Reform Act (BCRA). In *Citizens United v. Federal Election Commission*,[36] the Court, in a heated five-to-four ruling, held that the federal government may not ban political spending by corporations in candidate elections. The Court overturned a 1990 ruling that upheld restrictions on corporate spending to support or oppose political candidates and a 2003 ruling that upheld part of BCRA that restricted campaigning spending by corporations and unions.[37] The decision involved a so-called documentary, *Hillary: The Movie*, produced during the 2008 presidential campaign by a conservative corporation, Citizens United, which featured scathing comments and assessments of Senator Hillary R. Clinton's character and qualifications. Citizens United had lost a suit against the FEC, which barred the broadcasting of the documentary during the time restrictions imposed by BCRA for advocacy. BCRA banned the broadcast, cable or satellite transmission of "electioneering communications" paid for by labor unions of corporations from their general funds in the thirty days before a presidential primary or sixty days before a general election. The lower federal court determined that *Hillary* was nothing more than a lengthy campaign ad, and "susceptible of no other interpretation than to inform the electorate that Senator Clinton is unfit for office, that the United States would be a dangerous place in a President Hillary Clinton world, and that viewers should vote against her." The Supreme Court reversed a lower court decision, determining that based on the First Amendment freedom of speech, that government has no business in regulating political speech.

Barack Obama called the decision a "major victory for big oil, Wall Street banks, health insurance companies and the other powerful interests that marshal their power every day in Washington to drown out the voices of everyday Americans."[38] Obama further declared, in his 2010 State of the Union address, less than a week after the Court ruling, that it had "reversed a century of law." In fact, the ruling did no such thing. In 1907, Congress barred corporations from giving directly to candidates, and that prohibition still holds. Now, corporations (and presumably labor unions) may spend freely in support or in criticism of candidates for office, and the section in the BCRA which prohibited such activities during the thirty- or sixty-day windows before elections, was deemed unconstitutional.

Some dissenters fear that the Supreme Court ruling will open up a flood-gate of corporate spending in federal campaigns; others point out that corporations, particularly those sensitive to consumers of their products, may be reluctant to overtly oppose or support candidates. Constitutional law scholar Laurence H. Tribe pointed out that over two dozen states now permit unlimited corporate spending on campaigns, but without a corresponding rush of corporate campaign spending.[39] As seen in Chapter 7, however, corporations and labor rapidly began to take advantage of the ruling as they did battle in the crucial 2010, 2012, and 2014 congressional races.

The Making of Campaign Commercials

Twentieth century campaign advertising had the luxury of time. The campaign media team would write out its scripts for the candidate, there would be a couple of days of photo shooting, perhaps going to carefully selected locations throughout the state, getting the right visuals and theme for the spot. The candidate would read from cue cards or a teleprompter, voiceovers would be prepared, and perhaps in a week or so, the final commercial would be prepared. Filming equipment was still rather bulky and intrusive, and the film would have to be edited down to its final version.

Two innovations were added later. First, was the rapid-response ad. Pioneered by Democratic media consultant Frank Greer in the late 1980s, it involved preparing generic responses in advance of an attack by the opponent. Film was shot, voice-overs, music, and graphics were all in place, and all that was needed at the last minute was to fill in the blanks, showing how the opponent was wrong, or exaggerating, or lying. The innovation was in thinking and preparing ahead of time; but it still required considerable time to get the final product in place.[40]

The second innovation was to use qualitative research techniques—dial meters (electronic focus groups) and mall testing—to critique a commercial that is about to run. Up until this point, the campaign had to depend on the experience and skills of the media producer, with no feedback from actual voters. Dial meters, often called electronic focus groups or perception analyzers, are simple hand-held devices that can be moved from left to right, from 0 to 100. Each dial meter is connected to a central computer, and the response of each participant can be measured graphically, something similar to watching a lie-detector. Each participant's demographic data is stored, and it becomes possible for the survey researchers to determine, for example, that women over forty, have a much different reaction to a statement or image than women under thirty. The campaign may learn, for example, that the word "Republican" or "Democrat" is toxic with voters, so don't mention it in an ad; that the color of the candidate's sport coat is off-putting and distracts from the message; or that no one really cares about a particular issue that the campaign wants to emphasize.

Mall testing was first done by consultants Mark Penn and Doug Schoen when working for corporate client AT&T; later Penn and Schoen used mall testing for the 1996 Clinton reelection campaign.[41] They set up enclosed kiosks in shopping malls, asked participants about their political party preferences and other demographic information. Participants then saw different versions of a Clinton television commercial, and were asked to respond to the commercials and give follow up answers. The theory behind mall testing is that when most people look at videos in the mall kiosks, that experience is similar to the way they watch television commercials at home—by themselves.

There can be even more research conducted today using online surveys with embedded video clips. Coupled with greater sophistication of microtargeting analysis, it becomes much more dependable for a campaign to know if a video message will resonate with the intended public.

New Technology and New Breed of Videographers

Technology in the twenty-first century has democratized the tools of media production. There is no longer the need for a specially trained editor or an editorial studio. With sophisticated tools like Final Cut Pro and Avid, available videos can be edited on a desktop computer. Film is no longer needed now with the introduction of high-definition cameras, all digital, such as the versatile Canon EOS 5D Mark II, which boasts twenty-one megapixels full-frame sensor, and supports high-definition videos. This hand-held, lightweight camera is especially important for candid, person-on-the-street, or candidate interview *cinema verité* shots.

One of the best of the newer generation of videographers, Justin Germany, prefers the *cinema verité* style, and sometimes incorporates images from flipcams. "Old school guys wouldn't do this," Germany explained, "but we have a different mindset now. We mix and match styles, and put our work on YouTube, reality television, and web videos."[42] *Cinema verité* style goes beyond the slick, well-lighted, and well-produced media spot to creating a version that looks more authentic: handheld camera, rough cuts, poor lighting, herky-jerky quality, seemingly nothing more than an amateur (and thus credible) video production. This was evident in John Edwards's campaign for the Democratic presidential nomination in 2008. In launching his campaign over the Internet, he talked directly to voters, bypassing conventional news releases and television interviews, and asking that they join him in his crusade. Edwards, wearing a button down shirt, with his hair wind-tossed, made his remarks from hurricane-battered New Orleans, in a decidedly unslick production, aimed no doubt at giving his campaign a sense of reality and authenticity.

While web videos are one of the most important communications stories of the 2008 presidential campaign, they have not been able to replace regular television commercials as the dominant video communications vehicle. As Michael Cornfield has noted, "Web video did not supplant television as a political force in 2008, not by a long shot. Television's reach to voters who do not go online, and who go online but do not seek out political information, remains invaluable to campaigners."[43]

Direct Mail and Challenges from Email and Roboadvertising

Direct mail advertising can be traced back to Dwight Eisenhower's presidential campaign in 1952, and particularly to Barry Goldwater's presidential bid in 1964. With digitization, easy access and affordability of voting lists, direct mail became an important tool for campaigns starting in the 1970s. Persuasion direct mail is valuable at all levels of campaigns, from the presidential down to the local level, but it has proven to be most important in campaigns below the statewide level. Through it, campaigns can ask for money, persuade voters of the merits of their candidates, urge them to vote, and attack their opponents. It can also deliver a sharp, strong message—so strong that it wouldn't be allowed on television. Direct mail pioneer Richard Viguerie once said that direct mail "is like a water moccasin—silent, but deadly."[44]

Effective direct mail depends upon two critical elements. According to direct mail strategists Richard Schlackman and Michael Hoffman, "persuasion direct mail is only as good as the names you choose to mail to."[45] Further, mail must be attractive, interesting enough, and compelling for people, first to open it up, then read it and be persuaded by its message. Everyday, each household receives 1.7 pieces of direct mail (dare we call it "junk mail"), each vying for the attention of the reader. For political direct mail specialists, either through persuasion mail or mail soliciting campaign funds, their work has to be visually compelling, interesting, and written in powerful text. Above all, it must be noticed and opened.

Direct mail specialist Liz Chadderdon reminds us that while the average voter might have two telephone numbers, two or three email addresses, watch between five and 100 television channels, and surf through a similar number of websites, he or she will have just one home address. That address is recorded by the state board of elections, becomes a public document, and is available to list management and micro-targeting firms.[46]

What has changed over the past decade for persuasion direct mail specialists? First, there have been enormous changes in technology. Chadderdon, who broke into the business of direct mail in 1999, remembers sending ad copy and proofs to clients by fax machine. But now with email, Adobe format, high resolution digital images, the technology has "absolutely revolutionized" the industry. She can call on designers from throughout the world, have clients anywhere, and do all this better and faster than a decade ago, all thanks to improvements in technology. The second fundamental change is the advances in microtargeting, allowing the direct mail specialists to select targeted groups with greater precision and certainty. See Chapter 6 for further elaboration.

Despite all the online communication possibilities—from email to webvideos—direct mail remains a key tool for communicating to voters, both for persuasion and fundraising purposes. It has more competition, must work harder to attract its audience, but as Chadderdon appropriately sums it up, "new media isn't replacing old media; it's just more media."[47]

The Passive and Active Participant

The Internet and online communication are vehicles for the active participant, the person who seeks out information about a candidate or cause, who wants to give money, wants to volunteer, who keeps up on the day-to-day activities of campaigning. But campaigns have to reach other people as well: those not too comfortable with online communication, who aren't going to make the effort to look for election information, but still feel the motivation to register and vote. As veteran Democratic consultant Tad Devine observes, campaigns "must still reach that enormous segment of voters who are less involved than activists, but still believe that the act of voting and the choices made for political office are critical."[48] The best way to reach them, for the foreseeable future, is through television advertising.

In a similar conclusion, political scientist Stephen E. Frantzich observes that the Internet and its specific applications "are not a perfect match" for political campaigns. "Many campaigns get stuck in a broadcast model, assuming the Internet could be used like print, radio, and television. The Internet is not a broadcast vehicle but, rather, a destination tool. Individuals have to find one's website to use it. To a large degree, a user must want to go there. Unlike print, radio, and television, the Internet does not broadcast content to a broad audience, bombarding them with messages they might inadvertently be tantalized into absorbing."[49]

As candidates fight for the 2016 Republican nomination, we see television taking on an important role in highlighting some, tripping up others, and ignoring many. The first Republican debate was watched by the largest audience ever for a pre-primary event. Much of the interest was caused by the showboating and bluster of Donald Trump, who drew so much of the media's attention. Carly Fiorina, polling nationally at low numbers, received a boost thanks to her performance in the second-tier candidates' debate. Television has put the spotlight on Jeb Bush's passivity, Ted Cruz's temperament, John Kasich's independence, and the rest of the Republicans' inability to break through the old media's fixation on Trump. Hillary Clinton's campaign has been bedeviled by her State Department email mess and her inability to connect with voters, while Bernie Sanders, with a good deal of help from the old media, enjoys loud but narrow support. Despite social media and a wealth of online communication, it is still the old media of television that is proving to be the driving communication force in the 2016 elections.

4 Campaign Dollars

From Soft Money to Dark Money

We've marveled for years at the cost of elections, especially during presidential cycles, but [2008] is the first to cross the $5 billion mark.
— Sheila Krumholz, executive director, Center for Responsive Politics (2008)

With all due deference to separation of powers, last week the Supreme Court reversed a century of law that I believe will open the floodgates for special interests—including foreign corporations—to spend without limit in our elections. I don't think American elections should be bankrolled by America's most powerful interests, or worse, by foreign entities. They should be decided by the American people.
— Barack Obama, State of the Union Address, January 2010

Campaign money is playing an ever larger role in elections. Running for office in competitive districts is much more expensive today; candidates and their campaigns have to work much harder and longer to raise funds. Technology has helped, with the growing use of online fundraising. Thanks to changes in the federal campaign finance laws, outside groups were no longer permitted to use "soft money" to promote independent advocacy, but they soon discovered other means to channel money into campaigns. Many of the campaign reforms of the early 2000s were eviscerated by subsequent Supreme Court decisions, and after *Citizens United*, corporations, labor unions, and activists leaped to create Super PACs and so-called social welfare organizations that poured campaign money into elections. "Dark money" and fat cat contributors drew much more of our attention.

What Has Changed Over the Past Fifteen Years?

The Increasing Cost of Campaigning

The most evident change is that campaigns now cost more and more. The average cost of a winning House of Representatives seat went from $360,000 in 1986 to $1.6 million in 2012, an increase of 344 percent. During that same time, the average winning U.S. Senate went from $6.4 million in 1986 to $10.1 million in 2012, an increase of 62 percent.[1] The cost of some individual races in 2014 were astronomical. The North Carolina Senate race saw $120.7 million spent, with $37 million spent by the candidates (incumbent Kay Hagan and winner Thom Tillis), while $82.9 million was spent by outside groups. In the top ten House races, candidates and outside groups spent between $15 million and $24 million. Not too many years ago, a $1 million House contest was a rarity. Table 4.1 shows the expensive Senate contests in 2014.

Two observations on the most expensive Senate races in 2014: first, in seven of the ten, outside groups spent more than the candidates; and second, the extraordinary amount of money spent led to the defeat of five incumbent Democratic senators.

Costs of presidential elections have also surged during the twenty-first century. As Table 4.2 indicates, total contributions to presidential candidates have gone from $426 million in 1996 to well over $2 billion in 2012. The 2016 election promises to break all records, with hundreds of millions raised a good six months before the first primary.

The candidates in the 2008 presidential race raised a total of $1.8 billion, with Barack Obama collecting an extraordinary $745 million while John McCain raised $368 million; the remainder was given to the twenty-five other official candidates. Beyond the $1.8 billion raised by candidates, another $1.4 billion came from joint fundraising committees, the national political parties, labor unions, ideological groups, and a variety of other organizations, all trying to influence the outcome of the election. In all, Democrats collected about 59 percent of the money raised in the 2008 presidential cycle.[2]

In comparison to the $1.8 billion raised by the 2008 presidential candidates, just $800 million was collecting by presidential candidates in 2004. Of course, the 2004 contest was quite different from that in 2008: an incumbent president (with no challengers from his own party), fewer challengers from the other main party, and a much shorter primary cycle.[3] The 2012 presidential race saw the Obama campaign, the Democratic Party and allied outside interest groups raising a total of $1.107 billion, while the Romney campaign, the Republican National Party, and allied outside interest groups raised $1.238 billion.[4] The Center for Responsive Government estimates that when other presidential candidates, unreported outside contributions, and political party moneys are added in the mix, the 2012 presidential election probably cost over $2.5 billion.[5]

At the state level, campaign spending has also increased steadily from 1996 through 2008. As Table 4.3 indicates, all state candidates and political committees spent nearly $2.7 billion in 2008.

Table 4.1 Most Expensive Senate Races 2014 (in millions)

Race	Total Spent	Candidate	Outsiders
North Carolina (Incumbent Kay Hagan-D lost to Thom Tillis-R)	$120.7	$37.8	$82.9
Colorado (Incumbent Mark Udall-D lost to Cory Gardner-R)	$104.1	$33.8	$70.3
Iowa (Open: Bruce Baley-D lost to Joni Ernst-R)	$91.1	$29.6	$61.5
Kentucky (Incumbent Mitch McConnell-R defeated Allison Grimes-D)	$89.4	$53.7	$35.6
Georgia (Open: Michelle Nunn-D lost to David Perdue-R)	$76.1	$45.3	$30.7
Arkansas (Incumbent David Pryor-D lost to Tom Cotton-R)	$68.3	$28.5	$39.8
Louisiana (Incumbent Mary Landrieu-D lost to Bill Cassidy-R)	$65.8	$38.5	$27.3
Alaska (Incumbent Mark Begich-D lost to Dan Sullivan-R)	$62.3	$20.9	$41.4
New Hampshire (Incumbent Jean Shaheen-D defeated Scott Brown-R)	$58.8	$26.5	$32.3
Michigan (Open: Gary Peters-D defeated Terri Lynn Rand-R)	$53.3	$22.6	$30.6

Source: Center for Responsive Politics, http://www.opensecrets.org/overview/topraces.php?cylce=2014; accessed August 5, 2015; Federal Election Commission data.

Table 4.2 Total Contributions to Presidential Candidates, 1996–2012 (in millions)

	Nominal $	2015$
2012	$2,345	$2,437
2008	$1,813	$2,009
2004	$800	$1,010
2000	$529	$733
1996	$426	$647

Source: Federal Election Commission data, March 9, 2009; current and historical data compiled by Center for Responsive Politics, "Presidential Fundraising and Spending, 1976–2008," and "Stats at a Glance: Presidential Candidates 2008." Available at www.opensecrets.org/overview/index.php and www.opensecrets.org/pres08.php?cycle=2008; accessed August 15, 2009. Updated for 2012 election, http://www.opensecrets.org/pres12/; accessed August 5, 2015.

Table 4.3 State Campaign Spending for All Candidates and Committees, 1996–2008

	Nominal $	2008 $
2008	2,693,000	2,693,000
2004	2,129,000	2,407,000
2000	1,493,000	1,849,000
1996	305,000	414,000

Source: National Institute on Money in State Politics. Available at www.followthemoney.org/database/nationalview.phtml;accessed August 15, 2009.

At the state and local level, the costs of running for office, of course, vary widely.[6] In 1996, candidates for the state legislature in California spend an average of $328,000 (or $445,000 in 2008 dollars); by 2008, the average winning candidate for California Assembly seats spent $769,000 and California Senate winners spent $1,098,000. The state legislative races in Illinois ($106,000) and Virginia ($95,000) were the second and third most expensive averages in the mid-1990s.[7] But in a number of states, very little was spent on average in legislative contests: Idaho ($9,071); Utah ($7,047), and Wyoming ($4,172).

California, with its extraordinary size, population, and media markets, is truly the "Golden State" when it comes to campaign expenditures. Because of the great number of state-wide ballot issues voted on every election cycle, extraordinary amounts of campaign funds are spent on issue drives as well. For example, in 2008 alone, $477.7 million was spent on ballot issues in California. This was more money than was raised by the McCain-Palin presidential campaign throughout the entire country. In the past five ballot election cycles, from 2003 through 2008, interest groups (particularly Native American tribes) and citizens raised nearly $2.6 billion for ballot initiatives throughout the country, with California elections accounting for 62 percent of those expenditures, or nearly $1.6 billion.[8]

Gubernatorial contests vary widely in their costs, as well. In the 2009 Virginia gubernatorial contest, millions poured in from national party and other sources, and in this hotly contested race, over $58 million was raised. In the 2010 California governor's race, Meg Whitman, the former chief executive officer of eBay, spent some $160 million of her own money (along with another $20 million from others), but lost to attorney general (and former governor) Jerry Brown. Many gubernatorial contests, however, have much lower costs. Costs vary depending upon the size and number of media markets, the competitiveness of the contest, the number of candidates, and other factors. Altogether, the itemized contributions for state contests—legislative, executive, and ballot issue—during the 2009–2010 election cycle amounted to $3.8 billion.[9]

All in all, the cost of campaigning has gone up: dramatically in presidential contests, and steadily in other federal and state contests. For the 2008 election cycle, taking in all elections from the presidential contests to city council, about $8.6 billion was spent. But putting matters into a different perspective, columnist George F. Will reminds us that this sum was approximately equivalent to what Americans spent on potato chips that year.[10]

Federal Laws Governing Campaign Finance

There have also been substantial changes in both federal and state campaign finance reform laws during the past decade. Federal law regulates elections for president, the U.S. Senate and the House of Representatives. From 1974 through 2002, federal campaign financing was controlled by the Federal Election Campaign Act (FECA) of 1971, as substantially amended in 1974. Since then, federal campaigns have been controlled by the Bipartisan Campaign Reform Act (BCRA) of 2002. Several major reforms and changes, some unintended, came out of the new law. And as we shall see later, much of the federal law was eviscerated by federal court decisions.

Hard Money

The settled law, after the 1974 amendments and the *Buckley v. Valeo* decision,[11] determined how much an individual could give to candidates, political action committees, or political parties. Individuals could give $1,000 per election (primary, run-off, and general); $5,000 per year to a political action committee; $20,000 per year to a national political party; and a total of $25,000 per calendar year. Political action committees were permitted to give $5,000 per election (primary, run-off, and general); $5,000 per year to another political action committee (often a so-called leadership PAC); and $15,000 per year to a national political party. Because of *Buckley*, candidates for office were permitted to spend as much of their own funds as they wanted. This formula lasted from 1974 through 2002. Inflation ate away at these amounts: a 1974 contribution of $1,000 was worth just $254 in 2002.

Under BCRA, the hard money formula had changed. Individuals could now give $2,000 per election (primary, run-off, and general) with the amount indexed, so that in 2016, the contribution was $2,700 per election. The amount of campaign funds an individual could give to political action committees remained the same as in the 1974 amendments, $5,000, and was not indexed. Individuals could now give an aggregate of $123,000 during a two year federal election cycle. But as we will see, the U.S. Supreme Court in early 2014 struck down this aggregate limit in

McCutcheon v. Federal Election Commission,[12] leaving donors able to spend as much as they wanted, while still adhering to the basic limits of $2,700 to individual candidates, and other limits to PACs and parties.

In sum, the total amount of hard money, that is, money that fell under Federal Election Commission (FEC) regulation, doubled for individual givers through BCRA and was then indexed for subsequent elections. Still, to cover the $1,000 contribution under the 1974 amendments would require $4,840 in 2015 (rather than the $2,700 permitted under BCRA).

Soft Money

In the late 1970s, a new element—unlimited and unrestricted campaign funds, which were outside the limits and jurisdiction of the federal campaign law—was introduced through a FEC rulemaking and amendment to the federal campaign act. In 1978, the FEC created a regulatory exception, which permitted state political parties to use unlimited amounts of corporate or union funds (which were banned by federal law) to be used for voter registration drives, and later get-out-the-voter activities and issue advertising.

Then in 1979, the Federal Election Campaign Act was amended so that national political parties could spend funds on "party building activities" at the state and local level; this money would not count against the national party's hard money spending limits. Soon, this unlimited source of funding, outside the jurisdiction of the FECA, was dubbed "soft money." It expanded tremendously the ability of corporations, labor unions and other big donors to give unlimited funds to the political parties.

In 1980, the Republican and Democratic parties collected a total of $19.1 million in soft money; but by 1996, that figure had exploded to $263.5 million. Soft money, often criticized, became one of the principal targets of the 2002 campaigning finance reforms. The last year that soft money could be used was 2002, when $508 million was contributed to the national parties.

BCRA and 527s

The first important accomplishment of BCRA was to ban soft money for the national political parties, to restrict the use of soft money by state party committees, and to restrict federal candidates from raising or spending soft money. Overnight, soft money appeared to dry up. But just as flowing water will eventually find its way through the crevices of a dam, so too would campaign finance lawyers and politicos soon find ways around the soft money restrictions of BCRA.

It did not take long for political activists and fundraisers to rediscover section 527 of title 26 of the U.S. tax code. There have been so-called 527 organizations since 1975, when Congress created this provision of the Internal Revenue Code.[13] Such organizations, whether ideological, single-issue, labor union or business interest based, under the tax code were not required to declare their fundraising proceeds or list their contributors if the funds were used to influence the selection of candidates to federal, state, or local office. Here it was: a new, legal source for campaign funds, rediscovered through the tax code, rather than the campaign finance law. This became the new soft money, and the 527 organization became the new vehicle through which unlimited and (until July 2000) unreported campaign monies could flow.

During the 2002 election cycle, Public Citizen, a nonprofit consumer advocacy organization, tracked the funds that went to 527 political groups, and found that during the second quarter alone, $78 million in contributions flowed to them.[14] The 527 groups were not required to disclose how funds were received or spent before July 2000.

During the 2004 presidential election, 527 organizations blossomed. Democratic-oriented 527 groups raised $265 million, while Republican-leaning 527s raised $154 million. In all, $599.4 million poured into 527 groups during this 2004 election cycle. The Service Employees International Union (SEIU), through its own 527 organization, was the biggest contributor to 527 funding, giving $51.5 million in 2004. Further, twenty-five wealthy individuals gave a total of $146 million to 527 organizations. Some of the best known 527 organizations included Swift Boat Veterans for Truth (conservative, anti-Kerry, spending $13 million), Media Fund (pro-Democratic, $26.8 million), Progress for America Voters Fund (pro-Republican, $26.4 million), and MoveOn.org Voter Fund (anti-Bush, $4.7 million).[15]

In 2007, the Supreme Court, in *FEC v. Wisconsin Right to Life*,[16] reopened another path for soft money by broadening the definition of issue advertising (which is not regulated by BCRA) and narrowing the definition of express advocacy advertising (which is regulated by the law). It looked as though there would be a major increase in spending by organizations which would not have to disclose their donors.[17] In the 2008 presidential election, soft money spending did see a major shift in emphasis: federal 527 groups spent $200 million in the 2008 presidential election, roughly one-half what they spent in 2004. But the other organizations, 501(c)(4) social welfare organizations, 501(c)(5) labor unions, and 501(c)(6) business organizations spent "at least three times" as much in 2008 as in 2004 or 2006.[18] Unlike 527 organizations, the 501(c) groups are not required to disclose donors and only certain kinds of expenditures.

We will see in more detail in the chapter on Outside Voices how 527s, 501(c) groups, and Super PACs have become the new and potent forces in national elections.

Opting Out of Public Financing

In 1976, the system of public funding and financing of presidential campaigns went into effect. Taxpayers could make voluntary contributions and candidates could receive partial public funding during presidential primaries and, if they won their parties' nominations, receive funds during the general election.[19] As enticing as matching public funds may seem, strings were attached. For example in the presidential primaries, those qualifying for matching funds had to limit their primary spending ($37 million in 1996; $42.5 million in 2008) and to limit the amount of spending to a specified amount in each of the primary states. The state-by-state limits may look good on an accountant's balance sheet, but they cause havoc to the roller-coaster of real-life campaigning, where money may be needed to pour into a heavily contested early primary and a campaign would want to place all its bets on that particular contest.

For the general election, the nominees for the major parties would receive public funds ($67.5 million in 2000; $84.1 million in 2008). However, the candidates could not spend any more money than that and would have to cease their own fundraising. This restriction, however, did not prevent the major political parties from funding get-out-the-vote drives and party building activities.

Yet, candidates could opt out of either the public funds for the primaries or for the general election. Several candidates, confident that they could raise sufficient funds during the primaries, opted out of public funding: Steve Forbes in 1996, George W. Bush in 2000; then Howard Dean, John Kerry, and Bush in 2004. But Bush and Kerry, their party's choices in the general elections, both took general election public money. In 2008, Barack Obama's campaign broke the pattern. After publicly declaring that he would accept general election public funding if John McCain would do so, Obama backed off from that pledge, and became the first presidential candidate for a major party to rely solely on private funding since the public funding option system began thirty years earlier. McCain accepted the $84.1 million in public financing for the general election; Obama relied on private funds, and in September, 2008, alone, raised an extraordinary $151 million.[20]

Public funding for candidates in the presidential primaries could be a lifeline to second and third tier candidates who have not been able to attract and sustain large donations. But serious, big-moneyed candidates will forego public money and all of its restrictions, both at the primary and at the general election level. With unrestricted amounts of funding flowing into their campaigns, Super PACs and other groups, public funding has become an anachronism.

The Courts Step In

As seen in Chapter 3, the Supreme Court in early 2010 ruled in *Citizens United v. Federal Election Commission*,[21] that the federal government may not ban political spending by corporations in candidate elections. In overturning the BCRA ban on "electioneering communications" by labor unions and corporations during the crucial thirty days before presidential primaries or sixty days before a general election, the court characterized the ban as "classic examples of censorship." This is what Justice Anthony Kennedy, writing for the majority, said:

> The Sierra Club runs an ad, within the crucial phase of 60 days before the general election, that exhorts the public to disapprove of a congressman who favors logging in national forests; the National Rifle Association publishes a book urging the public to vote for the challenger because the incumbent U.S. senator supports a handgun ban; and the American Civil Liberties Union creates a website telling the public to vote for a presidential candidate in light of that candidate's defense of free speech. These prohibitions are classic examples of censorship.[22]

The prohibition of campaign censorship may have been the noble cause for Kennedy and the majority of five Justices. But Justice John Paul Stevens, speaking for the the four remaining Justices, blasted the Court's ruling as "profoundly misguided," noting that corporations and labor unions could have an unprecedented leverage in negative campaigns against legislators and that the integrity of elected institutions could be undermined. Stevens concluded that "a democracy cannot function effectively when its constituent members believe laws are being bought and sold."[23]

As seen in Chapter 7 on Outside Voices, wealthy individuals, corporations, labor unions and others have jumped in to the fray, taking advantage of the Supreme Court ruling as they geared up for the 2010 and 2014 congressional elections, as well as the 2012 and 2016 presidential campaigns.

Furthermore, thanks to the *Citizens United* decision, outside organizations and individuals can raise as much money as they want.

Corporations could now use their own funds and spend their money on independent expenditures. However, most corporations and unions decided to donate money to non-profit organizations, such as a wide variety of non-profit 501(c)(4) groups.[24]

An organization called SpeechNow.org challenged the $5,00 limitation that were imposed on political action committees and argued that independent groups, such as SpeechNow, did not pose a risk of corruption, and thus should not be limited in what it could raise or spend on independent expenditures. In May 2010, a federal district court agreed that the federal campaign finance law limits on how much independent organizations can raise were unconstitutional.[25]

Here was the one, two punch for freeing up campaign funds from outside interests: *Citizens United* opened up the unlimited spending for corporations, labor unions, and organizations; *SpeechNow* opened up unlimited raising of money by these independent organizations.

Super PACs

This led to the rise of Super PACs. During the 2012 presidential election, Super PACs played an important role. Winning Our Future, a pro-Newt Gingrich Super PAC, helped sustain the momentum for Gingrich even though he was having trouble raising his own money. Romney's Super PAC support came from Restore Our Future, while the Obama campaign was supported by Priorities USA Action. In all, each presidential contender had at least one Super PAC committee created, and by the end of the 2012 presidential campaign, these supposedly independent voices generated a total of $239.2 million.

During the hotly contested congressional elections of 2014, a total of 1,360 groups had organized as Super PACs, raising $696 million.[26] Each of the presidential candidates in 2016 has a Super PAC, or two, or three, that is raising money to support the candidate.

Dark Money

One of the fundamental pillars of the federal campaign finance law, drawn up in the early 1970s, was disclosure. If donors wanted to give money to a campaign, they would have to reveal their name, occupation, and employer. This rule still applies to hard money donations, but it does not apply to the donors to politically active so-called social welfare organizations, the 501(c)(4) and 501(c)(6) groups. This non-disclosed money was soon dubbed "dark money." It started off with a trickle with $5.2 million raised during the 2006 election cycle, but soon ballooned in subsequent congressional elections: $161 million in 2010, and $174 million in 2014. During the 2012 presidential election, $300 million in dark money was raised, and for 2016, the stakes will undoubtedly increase. Much of the money (69 percent in 2014) came from conservative groups trying to defeat Democrats. In 2014, when Mitch McConnell faced a tough re-election fight, $11.4 million of anonymous money was spent on his behalf,

Cory Gardner in Colorado was the beneficiary of at least $18 million, and Thom Tillis in North Carolina was helped by $13.7 million in dark money. The money was used for attack ads, for tracking opponents, digging up dirt on them, get-out-the-vote drives, and other campaign-related activities.[27]

Soliciting Campaign Funds

Asking for money is an integral part of any campaign. In the early stages and many times throughout the election cycle, fundraising largely falls on the shoulders of the candidates themselves. They have to make the "ask" themselves—calling up family, friends, political allies, and party faithful, speaking directly to them, asking them to help out by donating to the candidate. It is tedious, demeaning work. Candidates are also expected to personally show up for fundraising events, endure the small talk, rubber chicken, and fattening hors d'oeuvres, and have their picture taken with well dressed patrons. This part of fundraising will perhaps never change, whether a candidate is running for local sheriff or president of the United States: individuals giving money to candidates expect some level of the personal touch, at the very least a thank you note, a handshake and a signed picture with the candidate.

However, over the past decade, there have been some important changes in the manner and method of fundraising.

Bundling

Especially after the BCRA ban on soft money went into effect, the practice of "bundling" hard money became more important to candidates and committees. Individual contributors gather support from friends and associates, "bundling" their contributions together, and presenting them as a package. One of the earliest bundlers was EMILY's List, an organization that promoted women candidates for office. During the Bush-Cheney presidential campaign of 2000, some 241 well-connected individuals, called Bush "Pioneers," were responsible for collecting $100,000 each for the presidential campaign;[28] later, in the 2004 presidential campaign, there were Bush "Rangers" (collecting at least $200,000) and "Super Rangers" (more than $300,000). In 2008, Hillary Clinton's campaign was aided by 233 well-connected "HillRaisers," who pledged to raise at least $100,000 each; Barack Obama had 606 bundlers and John McCain had 536 such contributors.[29] During the 2008 campaign, the six leading primary candidates had listed over 2,000 individuals who bundled funds from friends and associates.[30]

There is nothing illegal about this activity and bundlers do not have to be identified separately in FEC reports. Bundling becomes an efficient way for campaigns to collect funds; it also raises the profile of individual bundlers, the "smart money" people who can open up their electronic Rolodexes and persuade friends and associates to donate maximum allowable funds to favored candidates. Thus, in 2012, there were 769 bundlers who gave $186.5 million to the Obama re-election campaign. The bundlers mostly came from law firms, security investment firms, business services, the television and motion picture industry, and real estate. By contrast, the Romney campaign relied less on bundlers, with only 106, who came up with $17.3 million, mostly from lobbying firms, finance and energy interests, and general business groups.[31] The reward for bundlers often is access to presidents (and presidential candidates), favors and special treatment, ambassadorships, and other rewards.

Online Contributions

Apart from the flood of money coming from wealthy donors, the most important change in the way money is solicited comes from the technology of online giving. For decades, the old methods of telephone and especially direct mail solicitation were the standard ways of contacting potential givers. Direct mail fundraising, however, is an expensive proposition. Consider the example of former lieutenant colonel, and later conservative talk show host, Oliver North, who ran for the U.S. Senate seat in Virginia in 1994. The campaign, through its direct mail consultants, sent out more than 13 million letters; 245,000 donors (or 1.88 percent—not an unusual rate) responded with $17 million in contributions. But the costs of soliciting those funds added up to $11 million, leaving the North campaign with just $6 million for its efforts.[32]

Expensive though it was, direct mail, however, was the life blood for most candidates. During the 1990s, more than nine out of ten congressional and nearly all Senate candidates used direct mail, not only to persuade voters but to solicit funds from them.[33]

In 1996, presidential candidates were just beginning to use the Internet to raise campaign funds. Bob Dole raised less than $100,000 online, but this was more than was raised online by incumbent president Bill Clinton. Campaign consultants considered Internet fundraising a very low priority during this period.[34] Then came Senator John McCain's 2000 bid for the Republican nomination for president. McCain won a surprising eighteen-point victory in the New Hampshire primary, and in the days immediately following, his campaign was energized by over $2 million in donations coming through his campaign website. Further, nearly 40 percent of the donors were first-time givers.[35] Republican consultant R. Rebecca Donatelli claims to be the first consultant to raise funds online, and was the chief Internet campaign consultant for both McCain's 2000 (where she raised $6 million online) and 2008 presidential campaigns (where she raised over $100 million online), and the Bush-Cheney re-election campaign 2004.[36]

In the 2004 Democratic primaries, former Vermont governor Howard Dean's campaign showed the promise of online communications. As discussed in Chapter 2, Dean made use of the early social networking site, MeetUp.com, to gather supporters. He was the first major presidential candidate to have a campaign blog and he tapped into the growing online communication revolution, particularly attracting younger voters. During the third quarter of 2003, Dean's campaign set a record in Democratic presidential campaign fundraising by gathering in $15 million; much of it from online sources and mostly from small amount donors.[37] The campaign also used direct mail, and was able to cut costs substantially by giving donors the option of making their gifts online.[38]

McCain in 2000 and Dean in 2004 gave a glimpse of the Internet's potential: an inexpensive, highly adaptive means of communication, available to long-time supporters and, importantly, to new supporters and contributors. The task of prospecting for donors, which was often a tedious, expensive activity in the days of direct mail, entered a new era, where the curious or newly committed could click on their support, adding their names to those who support the candidate.

The presidential candidates in 2008, particularly Barack Obama, raised the level of online fundraising to its present state of art. The Obama campaign adopted strategies routinely used in non-profit fundraising: asking donors to pledge on a monthly basis, asking supporters to raise certain amounts within a short, defined period of time, encouraging potential donors to contact friends and family, becoming their own versions of online bundlers. It challenged donors through a "matching" donations program: an individual would sign up to donate $25, but only if someone else would donate the same amount.[39] The campaign repeatedly sent email news reports, special messages from the candidate or campaign team, policy suggestions, and other information likely to both inform and encourage supporters—with all such messages having a pledge button, where supporters could donate funds. Social networking sites, web videos, and other forms of online communication also had pledge links. It became as easy and as convenient to send in funds to candidates as paying for products from Amazon, Land's End, or eBay.

Altogether, the Obama campaign had some 13 million names of supporters in its email files and sent over 1 billion emails, pitching them to different levels of financial supporters or potential supporters. Some 3 million donors made 6.5 million donations to the Obama campaign, totaling more than $500 million. The average donation was $80, and the average Obama donor gave more than once.[40] No presidential campaign in history was able to raise so much money from small donors as the Obama campaign.

While online fundraising was a key story of the 2008 presidential elections, both the Obama and McCain campaigns relied heavily on the old fashioned personal fundraising, with bundlers, fundraising parties, pictures taken with the candidate, all in the effort to capture campaign funds. As Anthony Corrado and Molly Corbett summed up, the 2008 campaigns "exhibited a panoply of tactics and techniques, from traditional high-dollar dinners to online matching fundraising challenges for low-dollar donors, special giveaways to sales of paraphernalia, celebrity galas to fundraising events held overseas, phone-a-thons to direct donations made through cellular phones."[41]

Giving to candidates and causes becomes so much easier with online contributions. On a Sunday, December 16, 2007, the campaign of Texas congressman Ron Paul, who was vying for the Republican presidential nomination, collected over $6 million online from 24,940 supporters. Trevor Lyman, a music promoter with no official ties to the Paul campaign and no prior political experience, created a website soliciting pledges for contributions to the Paul campaign. December 16 was the 234th anniversary of the Boston Tea Party. This online infusion of money was quickly dubbed a "money bomb," and surpassed all one-day fundraising records, until the Obama campaign's record haul.[42]

Giving to multiple candidates has been facilitated by partisan fundraising portal sites. For example, ActBlue, which dubs itself as the "online clearinghouse for Democratic action," has brought in over $128 million from its inception in 2004 through March 2010, with 420,000 donors giving funds to 3,200 Democratic candidates. The individual donation is approximately $100, and has ranged from presidential candidates to mayoral office seekers. One example of the effectiveness of online communications came in the forty-eight hours after Congressman Joe Wilson (Republican-South Carolina) cried out "You lie!" during Barack Obama's 2010 State of the Union speech. Within two days, Wilson's Democratic opponent, Rob Miller, garnered over $1 million from the ActBlue website.[43] A Republican portal fundraising site, Slatecard.com, with the tagline "It's fun to give *right*" had managed just $650,000 in donations during the 2008 elections and in early 2010 was getting set to relaunch itself for the 2010 mid-term elections.[44]

Online fundraising consulting firms have given candidates and causes considerable technical assistance so that they could capture contributions, build up email databases, and communicate effectively online with supporters. One such group, BlueStateDigital (BSD) was created in 2004, has had over 200 clients, including Obama for America, Wal-Mart Watch, Alliance for Climate Protection, and the Communications Workers of America. BSD helped its clients gather over $500 million in online contributions and capture tens of millions of online signups. For the Obama campaign, BSD collected 3 million individual donors,

2 million social network participants and helped advocate 200,000 offline campaign events.[45] Joe Rospars, one of the founding partners of BSD, became the director of new media at the Obama presidential campaign. In early 2010, former British prime minister Tony Blair signed on with BSD, which created a website, TonyBlair4Labour, to promote the Labour Party in its unsuccessful attempt at a fourth consecutive election victory.[46]

A 2012 Republican presidential candidate, Minnesota governor Tim Pawlenty ran an online contest through his political action committee, generating publicity and building name recognition for his own political future, and, probably most importantly, building onto his email list of followers and supporters. Colin Delaney, founder of Epolitics. com, argues that this is a smart thing to do. "It's a great list-building activity and there is nothing more precious to a politician than his supporter list."[47] This is an example of "crowdfunding" which is a subset of "crowdsourcing" (a neologism coming from "crowd" and "outsourcing"), in this case asking followers to help Pawlenty choose where to invest his political action money. A few of the Republican candidates Pawlenty was considering supporting asked their Facebook followers to vote for them. The winner gets to co-host a Facebook town hall with Pawlenty, send a solicitation through Pawlenty's Freedom First political action committee, and get a $1 match for every dollar the PAC helps the candidate raise (up to $5000).[48] Pawlenty's crowdfunding was a clever way to attract attention, but the Pawlenty campaign itself soon fell flat. It ran out of money, the candidate just didn't have the name recognition or appeal to keep going, and he soon dropped out of the Republican primaries.

In the 2016 election cycle, most of the attention during the first half of 2015 centered on donations from wealth sources. All presidential hopefuls had "donate" buttons on their websites and on the communications they sent to followers, but early in the game, many of the candidates found themselves gathering less money from small and medium-amount donors than the money that was given by wealthy donors to the Super PACs supporting them.

Who Gives to Political Campaigns?

Making a political contribution online, virtually unheard of a decade ago, is now a commonplace activity. It is an inexpensive way for campaigns to solicit funds and an easy and convenient way for contributors to give money. This might suggest that a greater percentage of persons now would be willing to donate money to political campaigns than before the online revolution.

However, even with the convenience of online contributing, the number of donors, both at the national and state levels, while growing, remains small. Following the enactment of the BCRA (2002), there was a surge in small donor contributions to the political parties and a decrease in contributions from large donors; but for congressional candidates and 2004 (and early 2007) presidential candidates, small donor contributions dropped, while reliance on large donors increased. Despite increases in small donor contributions, the Campaign Finance Institute concluded that the "vast majority" of Americans do not contribute funds to either candidates or political parties.[49]

Indeed, very few people give money. In a 1999 study of twelve states, the National Institute on Money in State Politics noted that the percentage of voting age contributors to state campaigns was uniformly small, less than 0.3 percent, and that of those individuals who gave contributions, a full 97.4 percent gave less than $1000 to candidates.[50]

Even in 2008, with a surge of new contributors taking advantage of online convenience, the percentage of adult Americans giving political contributions was miniscule. The most enthusiastic participation was for the Obama campaign: an estimated 3.1 million (an unprecedented number) donors were in its database; Obama received 69.456 million votes in the general election. Thus, 4.4 percent of those who voted for Obama gave him political contributions. More than 131 million citizens voted for either McCain, Obama or another presidential candidate in the general election; but another 81 million Americans were eligible to vote but did not.[51] Presumably, few of these nonparticipants contributed funds to any political campaign.

While presidential elections bring out millions who will donate money, it is quite a different story during congressional elections. This was revealed most starkly by an analysis conducted by the Center for Responsive Politics and the Sunlight Foundation of the 2014 congressional elections. Researchers found that among all the donors there were just 31,976—or about one-tenth of one percent of the total population of the United States. Together, they gave $1.18 billion in disclosed contributions (who knows about the dark money, undisclosed funds?). This represented 29 percent of all giving during the 2014 cycle, a record share. Who were these mega-donors? Mostly men, city-dwellers, who often worked in finance, and skewed somewhat more Republican than Democratic.[52]

Thus the real story of campaign fundraising is not the sheer number of donors, or the percentage of adults who donate, it is the impact of the wealthiest, who are making a major impact on both presidential, congressional, and other races. When 2016 presidential candidates had to file their July 2015 financial reports, we were given a window into the enormous changes in campaigning financing since *Citizens United*. Without doubt, wealthy donors are lining up to aid candidates. Sixty-seven mega-donors gave at least $1 million each, accounting for $128 million in support of Super PACs that were supporting specific candidates. This massive support from just a few multimillionaires was more than three times as much as was given by all of the 508,000 smallest donors combined. Altogether, twenty-nine Super PACs had raised $271 million from 9,500 donors, with an average donation of $29,000. Texas senator Ted Cruz's three Super PACs had raised $36 million from just six mega-wealthy donors. While the Super PAC supporting Jeb Bush, Right to Rise USA, had raised $103 million by July 31, 2015. On the Democratic side, four Super PACs supporting Hillary Clinton had raised nearly $27 million from 1,900 donors. This was still nearly six months before the first actual votes were cast in the Iowa caucus.[53]

While many of the wealthy contributors had given money to presidential candidates in earlier election cycles, many of those who had given vast sums before had not weighed in yet in 2015. Republican billionaires Sheldon Adelson, Paul Singer, and the Koch brothers, and Democratic heavy hitters Fred Eychaner, Jim Simons, and Tom Steyer had yet to weigh in.

5 Taking the Pulse of the Electorate

There is no doubt that public opinion research has become the central nervous system of the modern political campaign.

—William R. Hamilton (1995)

There's a growing problem of increased refusal rates, but a far bigger problem for the private polling industry is the competition from robocalls, Internet polling, and "quickie" polls.

—Paul Maslin (2010)

Professionally run campaigns at all levels rely on public opinion research to inform them of what is on the minds of the voting public. As Daniel S. Greenberg has observed, "politics without polling has become as unthinkable as aviation without radar."[1] Since the 1970s, political pollsters, their research tools, and analyses have become central to the operation of election campaigns. A well-financed statewide campaign will employ a variety of survey instruments throughout the election cycle: (a) a *benchmark survey* that gives a detailed first look at the strengths and weaknesses of the candidate, the political party, and the mood of the electorate; (b) *focus group sessions*, during which a small number of participants can explore questions and issues in greater depth; (c) *trend surveys*, which are taken throughout the campaign to gauge movement or change; (d) *dial meter analysis*, which is often used to test market commercials; (e) *mall testing*, which is used to gauge public reaction in a supposedly neutral setting, the shopping mall; and (f) *tracking polls*, which determine movement and trends in usually the last weeks of a campaign.[2]

Smaller-scale campaigns, with more modest budgets, will also use some of these services of professional survey researchers. In all campaigns, large and small, candidates and their consultants crave to know: what the voting public thinks, what its mood is, how our candidate stacks up against our opponents, what our strengths and weaknesses are. Without this information, campaigns are essentially operating in the dark.

What Has Changed Over the Past Fifteen Years?

More Polling Than Ever Before at the Presidential Level

During election campaigns, two types of polling take place. First, private polling, conducted by the individual candidates, political parties, and groups that are involved in or highly interested in the campaign. The information is not shared with the public, and is used for planning strategy and evaluating a candidate's standing with the public. Second, are public polls, conducted by colleges and universities, by public survey research companies on their own behalf and for television, newspaper, and other media source consumption. These are the polls seen in newspapers, television stories, and on the Internet.

Public polling has grown by leaps and bounds over the past decade, using traditional telephone surveys, online polling, and short automated telephone surveys. In the very competitive 2000 presidential election, between twenty-five and forty polls were being taken by survey research firms, newspapers or television networks, universities, and others per week. That year, there was increased emphasis on "instant" reporting and analysis. For example, just thirty-five minutes after the first presidential debate between Democrat Al Gore and Republican George Bush, the first analysis of the public was being reported on television. Television networks were letting viewers see focus groups and perception panels in action. For some, it made for interesting television viewing: a real-time glimpse of how citizens summed up the candidates. Instant poll results, from persons called immediately after the debate, were also flashed on television screens. However, there was also a price to be paid: a rush to report, with information from just a small number of persons. The National Council of Public Polls warned journalists that there was an increased likelihood of error in instant polls because of the relatively small response rates.[3]

By the 2012 presidential election, the number and rate of public polls had increased even more. Scores of organizations—some affiliated with universities, others affiliated with newspapers or television networks, and others were commercial polling firms—were regularly publishing the results of election or political surveys (see Table 5.1).

To keep up with those surveys made available to the public, several Internet polling portal sites were created, including FiveThirtyEight.com, RealClearPolitics.com, Pollster.com, and Huffington Post Pollster that tracked, and offered commentary on, the daily results of survey research and public opinion.[4] Several of these public surveys offered day-to-day tracking polls, conducted by automated recorded voice message (sometimes pejoratively called robopolls or robodial polls). Others were conducted through the Internet, while some pollsters preferred live

Table 5.1 Public Pollsters Tracking the 2012 Presidential Election

Polling Firm	#Polls	Aver. Error	Mode	Cell?
IBD/TIPP	11	0.9%	Live Phone	Yes
Google Consumer Surveys	12	1.6	Internet	N/A
Mellman	9	1.6	Live Phone	Yes
RAND Corporation	17	1.8	Internet	N/A
CNN/Opinion Research	10	1.9	Live Phone	?
Ipsos/Reuters	42	1.9	Internet	N/A
Angus Reid	11	1.9	Internet	N/A
CVOTER Intl/UPI	13	2.0	Live Phone	?
Grove Insight	18	2.0	Live Phone	Yes
Survey USA	17	2.2	Robodial	Yes
Quinnipiac Univ.	5	2.3	Live Phone	Yes
Marist Univ.	11	2.5	Live Phone	Yes
YouGov	30	2.6	Internet	N/A
We Ask America	9	2.6	Robodial	No
Public Policy Polling	71	2.7	Robodial	No
Gravis Marketing	16	2.8	Robodial	No
JZ Analytics	17	2.8	Internet	N/A
Washington Post/ABC	14	4.0	Live Phone	No
Pharos Research Group	14	4.0	Live Phone	No
Rasmussen Group Reports	60	4.2	Robo, Internet	No
American Research Group	9	4.5	Live Phone	Yes
Mason-Dixon	8	5.4	Live Phone	Yes
Gallup	11	7.2	Live Phone	Yes

Source: Nate Silver, "Which Polls Fared Best (and Worst) in the 2012 Presidential Race," *New York Times*, November 10, 2012, available at http://fivethirtyeight.blogs.nytimes. com/2012/11/10/which-polls-fared-best-and-worst-in-the-2012-presidential-race/?_r=0 (accessed July 7, 2015).

telephone interviews. Some of the more accurate pollsters using live phone interviews also incorporated cell phones.

As the above table indicates, there was a wide variation in the accuracy of the public pollsters in 2012. Some, like Google Consumer Surveys, RAND Corporation and Ipsos/Reuters conducted their polls through the Internet, and were quite accurate. Some of the best known, like Washington Post/ABC News fared poorly, while using the traditional live telephone interview, but not calling cell phones. Worst of all was the Gallup Poll, which relied on traditional interview methods. The candidates, political parties, and interest groups, of course, had their own private pollsters who analyzed the electoral dynamics for their clients. The questions and results are privately held, and very often probe different levels of attitudes, going beyond much of the "horse-race" aspects of many public media polls.

Shrinking Response Rate

While there is an increase in and greater reliance on both private and public polling, it is becoming more difficult to get people to agree to participate in telephone surveys. In past decades, the response rate was 60 to 70 percent, but now it is less than 30 percent, and sometimes approaches 20 percent in some states and metropolitan areas.[5] That means, of course, that in order to complete one full survey, four or five persons must be called. A high refusal rate means it costs more to recruit persons, adding to the expense of a completed survey. It also means it is more difficult to recruit the right demographic mix of respondents.[6]

Does the low response rate cause a non-response bias? Thus far, in the social science literature, there is no evidence of such non-response bias. While it is more expensive to capture respondents, social scientists Morris Fiorina and Jon Krosnick concluded that we "need not panic" about non-response bias based on lower response rates.[7]

Voter Lists Replacing Random Digit Dialing

Since the 1970s, survey research firms have been able to use random digit dialing (RDD) to contact persons. Computer programs can take all telephone numbers (including unlisted ones) from an area code or some other geographic location, and with the assistance of computer-assisted telephone interviews (CATI), efficiently place telephone calls. This breakthrough made it far easier and less expensive for firms to conduct interviews than to have individuals manually dialing the calls. However, with the widespread use of answering machines, caller-ID, call blocker, voice mail, and cell phones, and the apparent increased frustration and impatience of persons over unsolicited telephone calls, the RDD method of selecting calls has been called into question.[8]

In 2002, political scientists Donald P. Green and Alan S. Gerber proposed that RDD be replaced by clustered random sampling from voter registration lists provided by state election boards. The key here is that time and money is not wasted on those who do not intend to vote (as found in RDD surveys), and that a better sample of likely voters (who already have signaled their intentions by registering) can be employed.[9]

The benefits of switching from RDD to voter lists became evident to political consultants and campaigns: those who will be contacted already have a predisposition to be engaged in politics; a number of early screening questions can be eliminated (and thus save precious time for more important questions); and the numbers called will be the home telephone numbers, and there will be no wasted calls to businesses or other non-home numbers.[10] David Mermin, partner in the Democratic survey research firm Lake Research, notes that his firm calls from voter lists, where the phone number might be either a landline or a cell phone.[11]

Cellphone-Only Respondents

In 2004, the Lemelson-MIT Invention Index program asked American adults what new invention they most hated, yet could not live without. The largest percentage of respondents, 30 percent, said it was the cell phone, beating out the alarm clock and television as the most hated such device. Cell phones, of course, have become almost ubiquitous in the United States, and even more so in other parts of the world. In 1996, there were approximately 34 million cell phones in the United States; by 2011, there were 327.6 million, a cellphone for every person in the United States with 12 million left over.[12]

Increasingly, cell phones are not simply supplementing, but are replacing, landline phones. By December 2009, approximately 25 percent of American cell phone users relied on them as their only phone, and did not have a traditional landline; this number had grown from 3.2 percent of households in early 2003 that had only cell phones. Exit polls from the 2008 presidential contest found that 41 percent of young adult voters (age eighteen to twenty-nine) had cell phones only; for those sixty-five and older, there were just 7 percent with cell phones only.[13] Over 48 percent of young adults under thirty have cell phones only.[14] Cutting off the landline, according to veteran pollster Mark Mellman, appears to be a "lifecycle phenomenon: Those who are young, single, childless, living with unrelated roommates and mortgageless are much more likely to be cell-only, while older, married parents who own homes overwhelmingly retain landlines."[15]

For forty or fifty years, pollsters have relied on the landline telephone as a basic, relatively efficient and cost-effective method of reaching the public. With the growing use of cell phones, particularly among younger people, can pollsters shift to cell phone numbers while maintaining the reliability, efficiency and cost-effectiveness of landline calls? Public opinion pollster John Zogby and others have noted a number of problems with attempting to conduct survey research over cell phones. Cell phones, carried anywhere, might not be the most conducive vehicle to carry out a thoughtful conversation if answered in a crowded restaurant or coffee bar, on the bus or while stuck in traffic, while walking down the street, or in a classroom. The survey questions might be too intrusive, with respondents unwilling or unable to give candid and thoughtful answers, particularly if the questionnaire has thirty to fifty questions and takes up to twenty minutes to complete.[16]

Another problem concerns the "frame of mind" of the respondent. A cell phone user, asked to answer questions in an unsolicited survey may be hostile, impatient, or simply in a bad mood, if for no other reason than that the survey research firm may be eating into the cell phone user's available minutes. Further, is the problem of geography. When a landline is called, the survey researcher has assurance that the telephone is located within certain geographic limits, by the telephone area code. By contrast, cell phones go anywhere. Nothing illustrates this more simply than asking for the area codes from the cell phones of students in a university classroom. All such students live near or on campus, but they bring with them area code and cell phone numbers from a wide variety of places. Particularly when survey responses must be tied to a certain geographic area (such as a congressional district or state boundaries), it becomes difficult to gauge geographic location from cell phone users unless the cell numbers come from voter registration lists.

Associated with these problems is the fact that it costs far more to complete surveys by using cell phones than by landlines. For one reason, federal law prohibits the use of automated dialing, such as random digit dialing; thus calls must be conducted manually at considerably greater expense.[17] Some pollsters give a monetary payment to respondents to offset the cost of their cell time, adding to the overall cost of such a poll. It also becomes more difficult to screen cell-only respondents. Scott Keeter of the Pew Research Center noted in 2007 that his organization estimates that "interviewing a cell-only respondent costs approximately four to five times as much as a landline respondent."[18]

Another issue is that cell phone only usage is heavily weighed toward young voters. Keeter and his colleagues in 2007 looked at the question: "Does the absence of the cell-only adults create a significant bias in national estimates on variables of interest in social and political surveys?" They conclude that "The short answer is no, not now – or yet."[19] With the 2010 publication of the National Health Interview Survey, showing the growing increase in cell phone-only usage, Leah Christian and her colleagues at the Pew Research Center noted that, although "still modest in size" non-coverage bias "is now appearing regularly in landline telephone samples," particularly with landline coverage over-represented by older adults and cell phone-only coverage over-represented by younger adults.[20]

Social scientist Paul J. Lavrakas and his colleagues concluded in 2007 that the ability to gather reliable data is "being seriously challenged."[21] In April 2008, the American Association of Public Opinion Research (AAPOR) published guidelines for survey researchers who were attempting to reach respondents via cell phone numbers.[22] One of its conclusions was that high refusal, and thus the low response rate, "will plague" RDD surveys of Americans with cell phones for the "foreseeable future." A 2008 report by AAPOR concluded that the nonresponse rate in random digit dialing cell phone surveys is "somewhat greater" than in comparable

RDD landline surveys in the U.S. Lower response rates are also being seen throughout the world in survey research.[23]

Survey research consultants will have to grapple with the consequence of growing cell phone usage, particularly as they try to discern the attitudes and voting intentions of young people. Some problems can be mitigated, such as combining cell phone numbers with voter registration information, giving a geographic fix on the cell phone user. The questions of privacy and intimacy of the cell phone, high refusal rate, and particularly the high costs associated with cell phone surveys will continue to pose major problems. Nevertheless, as seen in Table 5.1, a number of public polling firms have incorporated cell phone numbers when they have made live phone calls or have used robodials.

Internet Polling

In 1998, the telephone was everywhere: nearly 94 percent of Americans had telephone service. But far fewer, just 26 percent, had access to the Internet, according to a study by the U.S. Department of Commerce.[24] Internet access soon became far more widespread, and with it came the first attempts at online polling. Some of the polls were nothing more than straw votes, popularity contests or ways to rally the faithful. During the 2000 campaign season, for example, the Democratic National Committee's website featured a weekly public policy "poll." This was the question for one week:

> As the nation approaches a new millennium, what are the most important priorities facing our next president? Saving Social Security, strengthening Medicare and paying down the debt, or implementing George W. Bush's $1.7 trillion risky tax scheme that overwhelmingly benefits the rich?

The question, of course, was misleading, full of bias, and pointing toward one conclusion only. Republicans decided to retaliate by electronically stuffing the website, resulting in two out of three responses favoring Bush and his "risky scheme." Democrats promptly took down the polling question.[25]

This kind of online-generated pseudo-poll became popular as people discovered the interactive capacities of websites and their public opinion questions. But there were more serious attempts and new business opportunities for legitimate polling firms who saw online polling as an advance over traditional telephone-generated surveys. Harris International, a firm created in 1999 by Louis Harris & Associates and Harris Black International did preliminary online testing of the 1998 elections. Another online survey research firm, Knowledge Networks, was founded by Stanford University professors Norman Nie and Douglas Rivers.

Pollster Anna Greenberg and social scientist Douglas Rivers observed that "Campaign 2000 served as the first great experiment of online survey research with electoral politics."[26] In the November 2000 elections, Humphrey Taylor of Harris International and his colleagues reported on the results of seventy-two races using online surveys. The results "exceeded our most optimistic expectations."[27]

Zogby Interactive, the online polling branch of Zogby International, debuted in the 2004 American elections. Pollster John Zogby touted his firm's ability to predict accurately 85 percent of the state-by-state races in 2004 and 17 out of 18 U.S. Senate races in 2006.[28] Douglas Rivers founded an online political and social research agency, Polimetrix, Inc. It developed a respondent pool called PollingPoint, a panel made up of 1.08 million persons. One of its projects was to conduct the largest ever state-wide election study, covering forty-four Senate and gubernatorial races. Polimetrix boasted of having a high degree of quantitative accuracy, "substantially better" than other U.S. firms. In 2007, it entered a partnership with YouGov plc, a leading British online market research firm.[29] During the 2008 presidential election, YouGov Polimetrix conducted online polls in all fifty states and the District of Columbia for CBS News. It conducted 31,148 interviews online, predicting the exact 6 percent spread of the final popular vote.[30]

There are several very attractive advantages of online surveys over those conducted by traditional landline telephone. *First*, once the considerable start-up costs have been absorbed (including the creation of a large pool of online respondents), there can be substantial cost savings over telephone interviews. *Second*, online surveys have a strong advantage permitting interactivity and multi-media functions. A political consulting firm, for example, may decide to show respondents several versions of a commercial it plans to run for a client. *Third*, there could be higher response rates. An online survey is less intrusive than one conducted over the telephone. The online survey can be completed at one's leisure, perhaps over a forty-eight hour time period, with the opportunity to review and change answers. *Fourth*, survey results could be compiled in real time and the results made available somewhat quicker than traditional polling. *Finally*, the online survey could involve a larger panel, perhaps 10,000 participants rather than a 1,000 participant telephone survey.

From the beginning, there have been serious questions within the professional survey research community about the reliability of online polls. In 2000, Murray Edelman, former president of AAPOR and then president of Voter News Service, dismissed online polling outright. His advice to journalists was, "the best thing to do [with an Internet poll] is just not talk about it, just don't give it any credence at all."[31] Veteran pollster Warren Mitofsky worried that online polling would "destroy the survey business" and because such polls were cheaper to conduct, they would drive out traditional telephone surveys, and result in "lots of data, but not valid data."[32]

One of the key issues is that the Internet and online access isn't available to everyone. As seen in Chapter 2, in 2009 about three-quarters of American adults said they use the Internet, with Internet usage above 90 percent for young adults, college educated, and those well-off economically. Internet usage drops with those who have only a high school education (39 percent) and with the elderly (38 percent).

Research firms who rely on online polling establish large databases of individuals from whom they choose their samples for each survey research project. Is the polling an accurate reflection of total population? Professor Robert P. Berrens and associates argued in 2003 that with appropriate weighting, Internet based polling can be a reasonable alternative to numbers drawn from RDD telephone samples.[33] In their attempts to solve this key problem, online survey research firms have spent millions to create large databases of respondents, from which they can select representative samples. Harris International has approximately 6 million persons in its worldwide database; Zogby International has 700,000; and Knowledge Networks has 50,000 panel members.

Knowledge Networks created a nationwide online panel, known as KnowledgePanel, which chose individuals from both random digit dialling (RDD) and address-based sampling (ABS).[34] Knowledge Networks boasts of being the only online panel that is representative of the entire U.S. population, providing a "statistically valid representation and coverage of many difficult-to-obtain populations, like cell-phone only households, African Americans, Latinos and young adults."[35]

Still, skeptics abound. A number of media outlets, like Hotline, *Roll Call*, The Rothenberg Political Report, CNN, and the print edition of *The Wall Street Journal*, generally don't use online polls. Nate Silver, writing for the *New York Times* in 2012, dismissed the methodology of JZ Analytics, John Zogby's firm, because he "did not consider their method to be scientific, since it encourages voters to volunteer to participate in their surveys rather than sampling them at random."[36]

Starting just a decade ago, online polling has grown to be a $2 billion industry, with the great majority of business coming from commercial enterprises. *Inside Research* estimates that just 2 percent of the online polling business is related to politics and elections.[37] The refinement of techniques and the major investments online survey firms have made in their online panels have helped mollify some of their critics. While several public media firms use online polling exclusively, and like Zogby, see it as perhaps the inevitable future, what about private pollsters, working for candidates, parties, and interest groups?

Commenting in 2007, Joel Benenson, Democratic pollster and later the lead pollster for the 2008 and 2012 Obama campaigns and the 2016 Hillary Clinton campaign, argued that Internet polling is "not yet viable. There are some uses for online polling, but it still misses out on too much of the population for us."[38]

Veteran pollster Paul Maslin, partner in Fairbank, Maslin, Maullin, and Metz (FM3), states that his firm does ad testing over the Internet, as a substitute for dial testing or focus group analysis. However, his firm doesn't do Internet polling per se. The reason? "Internet polling, for campaigns, is still fundamentally flawed. There still is a bias in the sample and self-selection," Maslin said. "We are still looking for a sophisticated analysis capability" using the Internet.[39] Rob Autry, vice president of political polling for the major Republican firm Public Opinion Strategies, stated, "What scares most political pollsters away from doing online surveys is the generation gap. No one uses them for political work, certainly not campaigns."[40]

Robo-Polling

Another form of survey research that has made substantial gains is the automated telephone survey, or as it is often called, robo-polling. Numbers are dialed automatically, and when a respondent answers the phone, an automatic message, not a live interviewer, asks the questions. The respondent then answers by pressing the appropriate key on the touch-tone telephone. The Rasmussen Report and SurveyUSA (which calls itself "America's Pollster") are two public survey research firms which conduct thousands of surveys each, using automated telephone polling.

Mike O'Neil of O'Neil Associates Public Opinion Research is skeptical of robo-polls, characterizing them as "cheap and untrustworthy."[41] It costs very little, he argues, to "throw a bunch of numbers into a database" and make automated calls using a recorded message. A number of media firms, including ABC News, NBC News, CBS News, CNN, the Associated Press, the *Wall Street Journal*, the *New York Times*, and the *Washington Post*, do not run polls that have not been conducted by live interviewers. Defending automated calls, Scott Rasmussen of Rasmussen Reports argued that traditional media outlets which shun polls like his were caught flat-footed by not recognizing the surge in support for Scott Brown in his Massachusetts upset victory in 2010.[42] Further, political scientist Gary Jacobson found SurveyUSA polls to "pass all tests satisfactorily" for quality and accuracy, when the pollster conducted 600-person surveys through automated calls.[43]

How accurate are automated phone calls? The National Council on Public Polls, AAPOR, and the Pew Research Center, among others indicate that the robo-polls did at least as well as conventional live-interviewer surveys in predicting election outcomes.[44] Some media firms do not publish the results because automated calls cannot exclude children from adult samples, and such surveys cannot randomly select respondents within a household. Most automated polls interview whoever answers first and then use quotas or weighting to correct for age or gender bias. The calls tend to be short, with no open-ended questions, and with no chance for a live interviewer to probe for a more complete response or to clarify questions that might be confusing to the respondent. Automated pollsters argue in their defense that respondents are more likely than not to give a more honest answer to a recorded voice than they are to a live interviewer.[45]

With Scott Brown's special election victory in January 2010, both robo-pollsters and traditional pollsters using live interviewers were correct on election day in predicting his victory over Martha Coakley. But ten days before the election, the robo-polling firm PPP and the traditional, live interview calls made by the Mellman Group and another by the *Boston Globe*, diverged by fifteen and eighteen points, respectively. Mark Mellman, president of the Mellman Group, uses this example to show how robo-polls, which ended up being right on election day, yielded vastly different results from traditional polling in the weeks leading up to the election. From Mellman's standpoint, "election day accuracy is not an unerring measure of pre-election accuracy."[46]

Brushfire Polls

Some consultants offer "quickie" or "brushfire" polls, which are conducted generally during the middle of the campaign to determine name recognition and to spot new issues that may have arisen. These are surveys with a limited number of questions, conducted over a short period of time, done over the telephone, interviewing a small number of persons, often just 300. VictoryEnterprises of Davenport, Iowa, for example, charges $5,750 for such a poll that, beyond the initial questions about demographics and likelihood to vote, will ask about five to seven questions of voters.[47] Susquehanna Polling and Research conducted a poll of 400 persons to determine who might replace the late congressman John Murtha in May 2010 special election for the 12th Congressional District in Pennsylvania. The brushfire poll was conducted by trained staffers using the telephone, but the margin of error, for a sample size of 400, was a very large +/– 4.9 percent.[48]

RTNielson Company provides a short poll of six questions, two minutes in duration, with 250 completed interviews, at a cost of $1,995, and a six-minute brushfire poll, with 300 interviews, for $2,995.[49] These and other short, quickie, or brushfire polls were used fairly extensively by candidates, political parties, and the news media. They were indeed fairly cheap, done quickly with presumably a rapid turnaround of results, but also came at a price. With just 300 interviewees, the margin of error is +/−5.7 percent at a 95 percent confidence level. A sample size of 400 or 300 hovers around the lowest possible acceptable numbers for a credible poll. By contrast a survey of 1,000 persons gives a margin of error at +/−3.7 percent. Given that the response rate may be only 35 percent, it would take over 2,850 telephone calls to reach and complete interviews with 1,000 respondents, but just 857 calls to reach and complete 300 interviews.

Everyone a Pollster

In 1998, an enterprise called Mister Poll was created, and for a time it dubbed itself as the Internet's largest online polling site. "Our database has thousands of polls on every imaginable topic from the controversial to the downright zany." On the Mister Poll homepage, in tiny print, it acknowledges that all content is for entertainment purposes only and on another page notes that none of its polls are scientific, but boasts that it has conducted over 100,000 polls since its inception.[50]

In 2010, pollster Scott Rasmussen launched a new venture, Pulse Opinion Research, which would allow anyone to run a poll, asking any question he or she wished to test. All it takes is $1,500 or so and a credit card number. "Tell us what questions you want to ask on either a national, state, or local level, and we'll take care of the rest. All at a fraction of the cost of traditional polling." A ten-question survey, on a state or local basis, asking 500 people would cost $2,000; a nationwide survey, asking 1,000 people the same ten questions would cost $3,500. Clients can write their own questions or use the pre-scripted templates. Regardless of the method chosen, clients are assured "the same level of quality and methodology."[51] But survey research demands careful attention to the order and placement of questions and to exact wording so that the questions neither mislead, confuse, or lead to a certain conclusion.

Another venture called Precision Polling allows people to enter their own questions, call a toll-free number, record the questions in their own voices, submit a list of telephone numbers and start dialing at 10 cents a call. Based in Seattle, and created by Gaurav Oberoi and Charles Groom, Precision Polling offers candidates the edge to "win campaigns with reliable data when you need it the most." Through Precision Polling, clients can conduct horse race polls, hot button issue polls, run surveys before and after big media buys, test their messages, mobilize voters, and refine and tailor micro-target mailings.[52] Oberoi told Mark Blumenthal of National Journal Online that a handful of survey research companies have already used his service to conduct political polls for campaign clients.[53]

Polling has undergone dramatic changes and stresses during the past decade. Random digit dialing, once the gold standard for selecting telephone numbers, cannot fill the bill, with the greater frequency of refusals, and the proliferation of cell phones. Economics plays heavily into both private and public survey research. Traditional landline-based telephone calls, using all the safeguards of scientific survey research, are expensive and time-consuming.

Political survey research consultants will still compete, but the traditional methods may soon be surpassed by automated robo-polls, quickie telephone surveys, online polling, and even do-it-yourself surveys. There will be more polling, but will there be better polling? We may be revisiting Warren Mitofsky's criticism: "lots of data, but not valid data."

6 Voter Identification, Contact, and Mobilization

In any election, there are only three kinds of voters: 1) voters who support your candidate, 2) voters who support another candidate, and 3) voters who are undecided. From this principle, all campaign strategy begins.

—Hal Malchow (2003)

Microtargeting is trying to unravel your political DNA. The more information I have about you, the better.

—Alex Gage (2007)

The one-size-fits-all approach to the world is dead.

—Mark Penn (2007)

These are the most fundamental and critical of campaign activities: identifying voters who favor your candidate, persuading them of your message, and getting them out to vote. Rarely can a campaign succeed without a clear understanding of its target audience and how to get them to the polling booth. Looking at each of these activities, we will see how there have been both profound changes in technology and metrics, but at the same time, see how time-honored shoe-leather approaches still are vital to the task of identifying and persuading voters.

What Has Changed Over the Past Fifteen Years?

Better Access to Voter Registration Information

The twentieth century methods of identifying voters involved reams of paper, check-off lists, data about voting history and issue preferences, and other information. Such efforts were often not coordinated or up-to-date, and failed to give a good picture of who potential supporters might be and how they might be approached. The old system also lacked reliable secondary data, such as lifestyle, demographic, psychodemographic information that could give targeters a clearer picture of potential voters.

The chief source of information about voters comes from voter registrations lists. These lists are public record and on file at state and county election boards throughout the United States. Campaigns, political parties, educational institutions and others can purchase voter files, although they generally are not for sale for strictly commercial purposes or for finding lost relatives. The contents of the files vary by state, but those available from San Mateo County, California, are illustrative.[1] When purchasing current voter files, a campaign or a voter list management service could receive the information listed in Table 6.1, below.

In other jurisdictions, the voter information may contain data on race and ethnicity and other characteristics. Since the late 1990s, states have undergone a transformation in the administration of voter information. Spurred on by the National Voter Registration Act (NVRA), the so-called "Motor-Voter" law of 1993, states have automated and integrated their voter databases. Michigan, for example, through its Qualified Voter File (QVF) project, placed into operation in 1998 an interactive statewide voter registration database that eliminated all duplicate voter registration records, streamlined the cancelation process, eliminated many time-consuming record maintenance activities, and cut down on errors and duplication.[2]

With the more sophisticated election files, readily available electronically, voter database management firms now have millions of records of voters in their files. One such firm, Aristotle, for example, maintains a file of 175 million registered voters. These files, which have to be continually updated, come from 4,000 election boards, county clerk offices, and state boards of registrars. A total of 3,100 counties in the United States maintain, to varying degrees, information about race, age, and vote history.

Table 6.1 Voter Information Available, San Mateo County, California, 2010

First name/last name
Residence and mailing address
Precinct number
Consolidated precinct number
Birth date and birth place
Telephone number
Date of registration
Permanent Vote by Mail voter status
Political party
Email address
Date last voted
Voting history for county-wide elections, 2002–2009

Microtargeting

Data management firms, such as Aristotle, can then add demographic and lifestyle enhancements to these voter files. Want to target voters who hold hunting and fishing licenses? Aristotle has a list of 5.4 million such voters.[3] Aristotle's enhancements, including the hunting and fishing licenses, are examples of the growing sophistication in microtargeting: using demographic, lifestyle, psychodemographic, and other data to enhance the information found in county and state voter files. Better data means better information on potential voters.

Ken Strasma, president of Strategic Telemetry and national targeting director for the Obama 2008 presidential campaign, stated that microtargeting "is arguably among the most valuable new technologies in political campaigns."[4] The data gleaned from microtargeting techniques can be used for get-out-the-vote and persuasion targeting, message selection, and fundraising, especially small-dollar donors.

Commercial marketers have used some form of microtargeting since the 1960s, and in the political arena, there have been list management firms that have sold a wide assortment of listings, often with catchy titles: Texas Christian Activists, Cream of the Crop Jewish Donors, Born Again Doctors Who Vote, or America's High-Income Donors.[5] Computer scientist Jonathan Robbin in 1974 created the Claritas "life-style" targeting clusters, sorting the 36,000 U.S. postal codes into forty clusters. The life-style clusters were given names like "Norma Rae-Ville," "Furs and Station Wagons," and "Golden Pond." The life style clusters have evolved over the years, and in 2010, Claritas, now owned by Nielsen, divides the American population into sixty-seven segments in its PRIZM segmentation system ("Shotguns & Pickups," "Park Bench Seniors"), another fifty-eight segments in its P$YCLE segmentation system ("Annuity-ville," "Fiscal Rookies"), and fifty-three segments in its ConneXions segmentation system ("IM Nation," "Landline Living"). Each segment represents between 1 and 2 percent of the American population. As an example, "Young Digerati" are characterized as "tech savvy and live in fashionable neighborhoods on the urban fringe." They make up 1.2 percent of US households, have a median household income of $88,728, are between twenty-five and forty-four years of age, are highly educated and ethnically mixed, belong to the social group "Urban Uptown" and "Young Achievers" lifestyle group.

In the 1970s, Pat Caddell, pollster for Jimmy Carter, used a very simple and not very sophisticated form of microtargeting by separating the electorate into regions and suggesting that Carter emphasize certain issues in specific regions.[6] Twenty years later, when working for President Bill Clinton's 1996 re-election campaign, pollster Mark Penn identified a group, which until then had been considered under the radar, known as Soccer Moms. These were mothers whom Penn described as "busy suburban women devoted to their jobs and their kids, who had real concerns about real presidential policies."[7] While most male voters in 1996 had made up their minds, independent mothers, who worked and raised their children, were still considered critical swing voters. Clinton sought out these voters with campaign promises to help the moms and their children: drug-testing in schools, clamp down on teen smoking, limits on violence on television, and school uniforms.

Democratic consultant Hal Malchow used some of the first microtargeting techniques in 1995 when he helped Representative Ron Wyden win a special election for the U.S. Senate seat from Oregon. Malchow's consulting firm developed a statistical technology, called CHAID (Chi-Square Automatic Interaction Detection) that analyzed how different variables would affect voter behavior. The CHAID program explored several variables, such as percentage of children in a neighborhood, ethnicity, and education levels to predicting voter behavior for Democrats, Republicans, and Independents.[8]

Microtargeting became an important weapon during the past decade, principally through the efforts of Alex Gage, long-time veteran Republican polling consultant, who co-founded TargetPoint Consulting in 2003. Microtargeting techniques were first field tested on behalf of Mitt Romney in his 2002 gubernatorial race in Massachusetts, along with contests in Texas and Michigan.

In order to establish the voter clusters and segments, there must be a considerable amount of front-end research. Several thousand probable voters are asked about their views. Then consumer marketing and demographic data obtained from vendors like Experian, InfoUSA, or Claritas are added into the mix. Then proprietary information held by the political parties is added, along with past voting history and fundraising records. Microtargeting researchers will then use a wide range of advance processes—such as predictive modeling, data and text mining, discriminate analysis, discrete choice, neural networks, CHAID, genetic algorithms, and support vector machine analysis, along with regression and factor analysis—to fill in the gaps and come up with the clusters and segments.[9]

Microtargeting was used full force in the 2004 presidential election, and TargetPoint was the exclusive provider of these services for the Bush-Cheney re-election campaign and the Republican National Committee.[10] In Michigan, for example, Republicans divided voters into thirty-one political categories, estimated how many voters were in each category and the likelihood that they would vote Republican. They identified 51,308 Religious Conservative Republicans and estimated that in this group 92 percent were part of the Republican base; they found 111,676 Tax Cut Conservative Republicans, of whom 79 percent would vote Republican.[11]

The microtargeting effort of Republicans in the critical battleground state of Ohio has been credited for making the difference in the presidential campaign. Both Democrats and Republicans spent considerable time and money identifying voters, but in the end, the Republicans out-hustled their opponents. As political reporters Peter Wallsten and Tom Hamburger of the *Los Angeles Times* saw it, the "new-and-improved GOP database helped Republicans begin to peel away select pieces of the old Democratic base, such as politically conservative blacks, Latinos, and blue-collar workers."[12] And, as Ohio went, so went the election, with Bush-Cheney defeating the Kerry-Edwards campaign.

By 2004, both major political parties had created comprehensive databases, with information on each of the 168 million registered American voters. The Republican database was called Voter Vault, and the Democratic database was dubbed DataMart.

Behavioral Grouping

One of the principal goals of microtargeting is to identify the base of the party's voters. Another tempting target is the persuadable or swing voter. Spotlight Analysis, a targeting firm that specializes in Democratic and progressive causes, developed a package to identify their core values and life styles. It took the 175 million Americans of voting age and grouped them into one of ten "tribes." Those tribes were placed on a liberal-to-conservative continuum of voters, with the more liberal "Resourcefuls," "Still Waters" and "Crossing Guards" on one end of the continuum and the more conservative "Bootstrappers," "Standpats," and "Civic Sentries" on the other.[13] While working for Democratic candidates, Spotlight Analysis crunched numbers on neighborhoods, purchasing choices, and family size. What the tribe members shared was not necessarily race or religion or other standard demographic categories, but a common feeling about issues and values: God, opportunity, community. Spotlight concluded that one of the groups, labelled "Barn Raisers," a group driven by moral (though not necessarily religious) convictions was key to the contest between Obama and McCain.

"Barn Raisers" were active in community organizations, ambivalent about government, cared deeply about playing by the rules and keeping promises, had less college education than members of other swing groups, and about 40 percent voted Democratic while 27 percent favored Republicans. They represented about 9 percent of the electorate. Spotlight's research found that 90 percent of the "Barn Raisers" voted for Bush in 2004, but that 64 percent voted for Democrats in the 2006 congressional elections. Using this targeting information, Spotlight Analysis client the Service Employees International Union (SEIU) focused on swing voters in North Carolina, Florida, Virginia, and Ohio. SEIU tailored its ads and messages to these swing voters, and asserted that independent analysis after the election demonstrated that the Spotlight behavioral targeting had worked.[14]

Mark Penn, who first identified "soccer moms," later expanded his analysis by identifying seventy-five "microtrends," some of which were, in his words, "big and obvious" but others "hidden, operating just under the surface." With these forces, Penn asserts, are the "seeds of unexpected changes."[15] Under the general category of "Love, Sex, and Relationships," for example, Penn finds several trends: the "Sex-Ratio Singles" (too few heterosexual men for too many heterosexual women), "Cougars" (older women who date significantly younger men); "Commuter Married" (married couples living apart for reasons other than separation); and "Internet Marrieds" (married couples who met online).

In one of the key U.S. Senate races in 2006, Democrats used micro-targeting techniques to identify 15,000 Montana voters who had never been contacted by the party before but who might be willing to vote for its candidate, Jon Tester. The Democrat was able to eke out a victory by 3,500 votes over incumbent senator Conrad Burns.[16]

In preparation for the 2008 presidential election, the Democratic Party and its union and progressive group allies poured millions of dollars into developing targeting databases. The Democratic Party under chairman Howard Dean created Vote Builder. But in April 2006, former Clinton adviser and veteran Democratic operative Harold Ickes, created Catalist, a private data management firm, with Laura Quinn, who headed the DNC data management unit before being swept out by Dean.[17] Catalist, serving progressive Democrats, provided data for both the Hillary Clinton and Barack Obama campaigns.

Heading up the Obama microtargeting effort was Ken Strasma and his firm Strategic Telemetry. Strasma described the Obama campaign as a two-year research and development project, "with the most aggressive testing of microtargeting models that I had ever seen."[18] The Obama campaign used Catalist along with several other voter databases. Two advances were especially relevant for the Obama campaign: the high quality voter databases and the quick turnaround time on voter file updates.

The Obama campaign used telephone IDs, asking hundreds of thousands of voters who they were supporting and how they felt on particular issues. This information, combined with demographic, commercial information and some proprietary methods was used to build statistical models predicting how others would vote.

Those in the microtargeting business concede that their models must be thoroughly tested before being used in the field. Alex Gage admitted that during the early 2000s, plenty of mistakes were made and that much had to be learned by trial and error.[19] Strasma noted that to test a predictive model, there needs to be a control group or holdout sample. This group, usually one-third to one-half of the total number of identified voters, would not be used to build the microtargeting model. Instead, the model can be applied to both the control group and those identified once the model has been sufficiently tested and shown to accurately predict voter response.[20]

The 2012 presidential campaigns took microtargeting to a new, unprecedented level. With hundreds, indeed thousands, of bits of information about probable voters, the Obama campaign was able to develop sophisticated algorithms to determine how to efficiently and effectively reach them. The program was called Project Narwhal and the canvassing component was called Dashboard. Digital technology expert Julie Germany called these two programs the "most revolutionary and least observable technology tactics of 2012."[21]

Advances in Voter Contact

Veteran Democratic political consultant Will Robinson described the two basic kinds of voter contact that dominated in the Twentieth Century Model: low-impact and high-impact. Low-impact describes (a) literature distribution ("lit drop"), placing campaign literature on the doors of houses of voters; (b) leafleting, similar to literature distribution, but in public places, like shopping centers; (c) visibility activities, such as yard signs, billboards, campaign buttons, bumper stickers, even human billboards. High-impact activities are (a) door-to-door activities, with political party or campaign workers talking to voters, asking for their vote; (b) candidate activities, which Robinson describes as the "most effective" form of voter contact: the candidate directly asking voters for their support, face-to-face; (c) precinct captains, a usually effective method, relying on neighbors and friends to persuade voters; (d) direct mail; and (e) phone banks.[22]

All of these activities, both high-impact and low-impact, remain fundamental in twenty-first century campaigns as well. No matter the electronic sophistication and microtargeting wizardry, shoe leather, handshakes, and personal contact still are the most important aspects of the ground game of electoral politics. What has been added over the past decade, however, has been the overlay of technology and pinpoint targeting to much more accurately connect with likely voters.

Email and Text Messaging

By the beginning of this century, campaigns were finding email an inexpensive vehicle for communicating with voters. Early on, candidates were warned by professionals not to simply blast emails, hoping to cover as many people as possible, but also running the risk of irritating voters more than enlightening them. Email became a much more potent vehicle once it became associated with other targeted information: ZIP code, address, voting history, party affiliation and more. By 2000, the Republican National Committee was the first political party to have amassed a million email addresses.

By the 2004 presidential campaign, email files helped persuasion, fundraising, and get-out-the-vote efforts come into their own. The Bush-Cheney re-election campaign boasted of some 6 million email addresses. The Republican National Committee sent millions of emails to voters attacking the Democratic nominee for president John Kerry. The Bush-Cheney campaign had some 1 million subscribers to its electronic news-letters, while the Kerry-Edwards campaign claimed some 2 million subscribers.[23]

Former Arkansas governor Mike Huckabee, running for the Republican nomination for president in 2008 (and once again in 2016), was aided by a massive email list of conservative Christian voters. The list was compiled by a physician from Montgomery, Alabama, named Randy Brinson, who had created an organization called Redeem the Vote, a non-partisan, non-profit voter registration organization. The list apparently had 71 million contacts and was developed as a spin off from those who had seen Mel Gibson's movie, *The Passion of the Christ.* James Caviezel, the actor who portrayed Jesus, assisted Redeem the Vote by making a video that was distributed by electronic mail to more than 60 million people.

Huckabee used the email list in Iowa, hiring Webcasting TV to manage the list, and came up with 414,000 potential contacts in Iowa.[24] What was done here is contact the old fashioned way: reaching out to voters one at a time, but focusing carefully on a highly favorable audience: Iowa conservative Christian voters. In the end, Huckabee received 40,954 caucus votes, representing 35 percent of the Republican vote, giving him first place and 17 of the 34 delegates available.

The best use of email, text messaging, and for that matter, all aspects of Web 2.0 deployment, comes from the Obama 2008 and 2012 campaigns. The 2008 campaign gathered over 13 million email addresses and altogether sent out 7,000 unique email messages. Once in a while, all 13 million followers would get the same email, but most were targeted to specific audiences: the person who had given $25 to the campaign was asked in a subsequent email to give perhaps $50; the Obama supporter interested in environmental issues got emails tailored to that concern; those who opened up their email in the morning (and there are ways of knowing this) got their Obama emails in the morning. Most of the emails had a "donate" button attached, and many also were accompanied by a video. Campaign research showed that viewers looked at the email for a longer time (and perhaps absorbed its message better) when it was accom-panied by a video.[25]

During the 2006 congressional elections, political scientists Allison Dale and Aaron Strauss conducted a study to determine the effectiveness of text messaging as a get-out-the-vote tool. They found that text messaging could be an effective mobilization tool, that boosted voter turnout by 3 percentage points. They also found that while there was some annoyance from participants, text messaging was the preferred method of reaching them (31 percent), even more preferable than by email (30 percent), in person (6 percent), or through a cell phone call (2 percent). Further, a study by the New Voters Project estimated an increase of voter turn out by 4 percent and found that text messaging, rather than door-to-door contact or phone banks, was far less expensive: costing $1.56 per vote for text messaging, but $20 to $30 per vote for phone banking or door-to-door canvassing.[26]

The 2008 Obama campaign vigorously went after cell phone numbers. Followers at rallies were encouraged to use their cell phones to text the campaign and receive messages in return. When the campaign was about to announce that Senator Joe Biden had been chosen as Obama's running mate, it saw an opportunity to boost the number of cell phone numbers it had in its database. Supporters were encouraged to sign up for first notice of the Biden decision, and through this encouragement, the campaign was able to increase by fifteen fold the number of cell phones it had in its database. They were also encouraged to watch the first big public announcement on www.BarackObama.com rather than going to CNN or other news sources. While at the site, the viewer could sign up to volunteer, learn more about Biden, and, of course, donate money.

By 2012, the Federal Election Commission permitted the presidential campaigns to accept donations through text messages. Obama supporters could text the word GIVE to 62262 (spelling out Obama) while Romney supporters could text GOMITT (466488).[27]

Reaching Supporters by Smart Phone Applications

One of the key attractions of the Apple iPhone, first introduced in 2007, was the applications feature. Hundreds, then thousands, of businesses and entrepreneurs created applications for all sorts of interests, including politics. The Obama '08 campaign released a free application for iPhones and iPodtouch. The application allows Obama supporters to have the campaign at their fingertips. A "Call Friends" section assists volunteers in calling their friends to support Obama. The volunteers' contacts are prioritized by key battleground states. A "Call Stats" section lets the viewers see how their call totals compare with those of leading callers. The "Get Involved" section directs the viewers to their local Obama for America headquarters. Viewers can also receive updates from the campaign through text messaging or email. They can browse national and local campaign coverage, find the location and time of events, view videos and photos from the campaign, and in a section called "Issues" get information about Obama and Biden's essential issues facing the United States.[28]

A powerful, efficient way to canvass voters comes from the combination of mobile smart phone technology, phone applications, and voting lists. One example is "Ground Game," a cell phone application created by a joint partnership of Moonshadow Mobile, a mobile technology company, and Labels & Lists, Inc., a voter list management firm. Ground Game uses Google map technology, with an overlay of voter history, to give a graphic, visually powerful picture of where voters live and how they voted in the past.

Readers familiar with smart phone applications (like those found in iPhone, Android, and others) know how they can pinpoint restaurants, grocery stores, or gas stations on a Google map. The same principle applies in Ground Game, with voters identified by party preference, voting history, and other information stored by local or state election officials. A campaign volunteer can go to a particular precinct and know which doors to knock on. A Republican campaign, for example, might want to contact all reliable Republican voters, those who occasionally vote Republican, and those independents who might be persuaded to join up. The volunteer canvasser might, after talking to the persons at the address, determine that they are strongly Republican and intend to vote for the candidate, or are sitting on the fence and need further information and perhaps follow up telephone calls. As the canvasser finishes one house, she can then relay the information back to campaign headquarters using her cell phone.[29]

This kind of detailed ground work—identifying likely voters, determining how strong they are in their convictions, noting whether they need a ride to the polling station—has always been the bread and butter of a field campaign. Now, the paper records and reports, the haphazard updating of voting records, and all the inefficiencies found in past canvassing have been supplanted by the technological efficiencies of smart phones and digital records and analysis.

Individual candidates in 2010 are following the lead of Obama 08 and creating their own iPhone applications. For example, Republican candidates Chuck DeVore, who ran in the primary for the California Senate seat, and Liz Carter, running as a candidate for the fourth congressional district in Georgia, used iPhone applications to showcase their campaign information, policy issues, photos, events, and allowing supporters to volunteer for the campaign, contribute money, and share information with their friends using Twitter and Facebook. The iPhone applications, called MyPolitics, were created jointly by RaiseDigital and Purple Forge, two new media consulting firms.

The 2012 Obama campaign introduced a Canvass feature on its Obama for America app, giving supporters access to homes near where they lived, and gave them the opportunity to canvass with greater efficiency and purpose. The Romney campaign introduced its own app, With Mitt. But the Obama app proved to be far more useful, enabling a massive voter turnout effort on Election Day.

Another innovative feature found in the 2012 Obama campaign was a program called "Optimizer." Using its vast knowledge of individual voters, the campaign was able to target cable television viewers who were watching at off hours, say 1:00 a.m. and were susceptible to Obama's message. Instead of broadcasting, this was narrow casting at its most productive. Buying cheap advertising time on less than popular cable stations at odd times, hoping to reach likely supporters.

Household-Addressable Advertising

Direct mail for years has refined its advantage: the ability to pinpoint individual voters by mailbox. Now at least 20 million homes that subscribe to DIRECTV and DISH Network will also be targeted, just like direct mail customers. With the extraordinary amount of information known about cable subscribers (what they watch, when they watch) coupled with the vast consumer and voter information compiled on them, it will be even easier for campaigns to reach just the right voter. For example, in Apartment 615, the thirty-year-old female first time voter with a high school education who owns a used Honda Fit could get an entirely different political commercial while she watches "Modern Family," than would the sixty-two-year-old divorced woman living next door in Apartment 617, who sometimes votes, and is also watching the same episode of "Modern Family."[30]

The Challenges and Opportunities of Early Voting

In 1998, citizens in Oregon approved the Vote by Mail initiative and transformed the way they elect public officials. Ballots and official election guides are mailed between fourteen and eighteen days before an election to the address of registered voters. Oregonians have two weeks to return the ballot through the mail or at official drop-off sites. Voters must sign the outside of the envelope and their signatures are checked against records on file at the state elections office. It is a very popular measure, and state officials tout its accomplishments: mail-in only means no polling stations (and all the expenses associated with training poll workers and site preparation), much higher voter participation, convenience of voting when one has the time, the educational benefits of studying the issues before voting, a built-in paper trail and a reduction of voter fraud.[31] It is a decidedly low-tech, simple solution, to problems made evident by Florida's "hanging chads" in 2000, periodic breakdowns of electronic voting machines, and exasperatingly long lines to vote at polling stations.

By 2014, Oregon was joined by Washington state and Colorado in adopting mail-in only voting. But by 2014, thirty states had adopted another reform, no-excuse absentee ballot voting. This meant that the traditional way of viewing the election—as a "one day sale" on Election Day in early November—had been fundamentally changed. During the 2000 and 2004 presidential elections, early voters tended to be better educated, older, with higher incomes and Republican. This changed in 2008: early voters were younger, more African-American, and more Democratic. In 2008 voting began in late September with Iowa voters casting ballots on the 23rd, and Ohio voters able to make their selections on the 30th; and by Election Day, 16 million persons (or 13 percent of the total) had voted early.[32] During the 2012 campaign, both the Obama and Romney campaigns adjusted their general election schedules, rearranged advertising plans and voter contact programs in order to capture those early voters. Every vote was critical and both sides worked hard to capture both early and Election Day voters.

When voters cast their vote early, either through mail-in or absentee ballots, how do you eliminate them from future voter contact calls? Bob Blaemire of Catalist, the voter contact company hired by the Obama for America campaign, explained that in twenty-three states, volunteers and local staffers would pick up information from county election officials to determine who had voted. That information was uploaded nightly into the Catalist tracking system, and the names of persons who had already voted would be matched with existing voter data information and would be eliminated from the upcoming voter contact lists.[33]

Early voting also changes a campaign's timing and planning. Mike DuHaime, political director for John McCain explained that with early voting "Election Day can be spread out over weeks. That means your get-out-the-vote costs are more than ever."[34] The trend toward more early, no-excuses voting will most likely increase, with more and more voters opting out of the traditional Election Day poll booths.

Automated Telephone Calls (Robocalls) and Push-Polling

Robocalls, the automated telephone calls that are sent to thousands, sometimes millions, of voters, have become a weapon of choice for many campaigns during the past decade. During the 2006 congressional elections, 64 percent of persons interviewed said that they had been contacted by automated telephone messages during the last critical weeks of the campaign.[35] In the months leading up to the 2008 Iowa caucuses,

81 percent of Iowans surveyed by the Pew Research Center said they had received a robocall; 68 percent of New Hampshire voters said they had received such calls.[36]

The chief attraction of robocalls is that they are far less expensive than direct mail, regular telephone calls, or television advertising and they can be sent quickly and efficiently through computer-generated software systems.[37] Mark Hampton said that his firm, robodial.org, had made more than 2 million robocalls for Democrats in 2007, at 2 cents per call; this compares favorably to direct mail, costing 50 cents per piece of mail.[38]

One telephone firm, PoliticalCalling.com, touts a software system called VirtualCall, which "hears" the response at the other end of the message. The system can determine, with 98 percent accuracy, if the message is picked up by an answering machine, a fax number, a busy signal, and an actual person answering the phone. The software can also determine that if there are busy signals or unanswered calls at a certain time of day, then the calls can be redirected to another time. The software is also capable of personalizing each call with a constituent or voter's name: "Hi Jim, sorry I missed you at home, this is Tiffany from the Tom Richards for governor campaign."[39]

Thanks to advancements in telephone software technology, robocalls were widely used in campaigns during the last decade. The automated calls can be used to get out the vote, notify voters of absentee ballots, make advocacy calls, deliver persuasion messages, remind people to vote, leave information for volunteers, and solicit funds. Robocalls can also transfer the listener to a live operator or to the office of a legislator or candidate ("Press 1 to be connected directly to Congressman Smith's office"), called "patch-through" calls.

Here's an example of a thirty-second persuasion robocall placed by the Republican National Committee and the McCain-Palin campaign during the 2008 presidential election:

> Hello. I'm calling for John McCain and the RNC because you need to know that Barack Obama has worked closely with domestic terrorist Bill Ayers, whose organization bombed the U.S. Capitol, the Pentagon, a judge's home, and killed Americans. And Democrats will enact an extreme leftist agenda if they take control of Washington. Barack Obama and his Democratic allies lack the judgment to lead our country. This call was paid for by McCain-Palin 2008 and the Republican National Committee, at 202-863-8500.[40]

Robocalls, cost-efficient and technologically easy to conduct, can also be highly annoying and even counterproductive. The calls can be informative and positive; they can also be intimidating and threatening. Dinners are interrupted and evenings spoiled by relentless telephone messages. Woe be unto the voter who lives in a battleground state or a heavily contested congressional district during the last several weeks or months of the campaign, who is bombarded daily and nightly by automated calls. With robocalls, voters are paying the price for automation and techno-logical advancement. *Orange County Register* columnist David Whiting struck a chord with many when he wrote, "Politicians' robocalls drive me nuts."[41]

A pernicious variant of automated calls is the push-poll. Push-polling has nothing to do with legitimate polling, and probably would be better called by other names: negative advocacy, persuasion calls, or vote suppression calls.[42] Push-polls are usually done in the final week of the campaign, under the guise of a short series of questions, and they usually last no more than 30 to 60 seconds. For example, "Would you vote for Congressman Smith if you knew he lied about his military service record?" Push-polling calls flourished in the 1990s, and even though they have been condemned by the American Association of Political Consultants (AAPC) and the principal survey research organizations, they have been used widely in the 2000s. Still in 2010, firms like PoliticalCalling.com and WinningCalls.com state on their websites that they offer such services.

In response to complaints from citizens and groups, several states have enacted legislation restricting automated telephone calls. But what has resulted is a patchwork of laws: twenty-three states and the District of Columbia have no restrictions; eleven states have disclosure requirements, time limits, or regulations on push polls; fourteen states have either Do Not Call lists, require live operators, or impose a fee; and two states (Wyoming and Arkansas) impose severe penalties for robocalls for non-emergency purposes.[43] A number of proposals have been submitted to Congress in recent years to regulate political robocalls on a nationwide basis, including time restrictions (usually not before 8:00 a.m. and after 9:00 p.m.), requiring disclosure of the sponsor at the beginning of the message, and permitting state attorneys general to provide injunctive relief, and other measures.[44] However, there is currently no federal legis-lation regulating or prohibiting political automated telephone calls.[45]

One of the central problems of adding political automated calls to the nationwide Do Not Call Registry for commercial calls, which now include 150 million telephone numbers, or restricting the calls in other ways, is that such actions could bump up against the First Amendment freedom of speech. From a practical standpoint, banning or restricting robocalls might also take away from underfunded candidates one of the least expensive ways to communicate with voters.

With a patchwork of state laws and no federal law, some citizens have taken the matter of political robocalls into their own hands. A National

Political Do Not Contact Registry (NPDNC) has been created; it is a non-partisan grassroots organization to "take control back by asking our elected representatives to *stop calling us at home*." Its website, Stoppoliticalcalls.org claims that there are 120,000 members on the NPDNC list (who have paid $24.99 to register), and that that database is distributed to candidates, political action committees, advocacy groups and other groups urging them not to call the individuals on the list. The organization also tries to spread the word that robocalls are in fact ineffective and negatively impact on the lives of those who receive them.[46]

Do robocalls, email, and other communications actually work? Social scientists Donald Green and Alan Gerber, in the second edition of their book *Get Out the Vote: How to Increase Voter Turnout*,[47] look at a number of get-out-the-vote tools to try to get voters to the polls: door-to-door canvassing, leafleting, direct mail (both partisan and non-partisan), phone bank volunteer, professional phone banking, robocalls, email, election day festivals, television, and radio. They argue that direct mail and robocalls for GOTV purposes are relatively ineffective and that the capacity of direct mail to mobilize voters is "relatively limited" and that "there is no synergy between mail and other GOTV tactics." Green and Gerber conclude that email is an expensive investment for the return: calling the cost estimate for mass e-mails "rather dismal."[48]

Gerry Tyson, who heads a Texas Democratic firm that does robocalls, argues that Green and Gerber don't do justice to the method of targeting as now practiced. Robocalls aren't done in isolation. "Statistically speaking," Tyson argues, "[robocalls] probably do have little effect when used in isolation. But used in combination with other forms of outreach, there is little doubt robocalls are effective."[49]

The Service Employees International Union (SEIU) found that nothing worked better than persuasion phone calls delivered by actual people. The SEIU spent in excess of $80 million to influence the 2008 election, contacting more than 4.5 million voters in ten battleground states.[50] In its effort, SEIU relied on telephone calls for 64 percent of their voter contact and for 24 percent of their neighborhood canvasses. The union was able to pay hundreds of members to make calls full time. According to Jon Youngdahl, the SEIU's national political director, "text messaging and face to face contact are really keys to success." He argues that robocalls don't work for get-out-the-vote drives; perhaps as persuasion tools, but not for GOTV.

Get-Out-The-Vote: 72 Hours and Beyond

For years, Republicans complained that they could not keep up with labor unions and liberal groups aligned with the Democratic Party in getting their voters to the polls. While Bush and the Republicans barely won the 2000 presidential campaign, it was evident that they were being out-hustled by Democratic supporters in their get-out-the-vote efforts. With the urging of White House senior political operatives Karl Rove and Ken Mehlman, and Republican National Committee chairman Jack Oliver, the 72-Hour Project was born. Named for the seventy-two critical hours before election day, the project was the culmination of an eighteen-month effort headed by Blaise Hazelwood, political director of the RNC, and intended to get the party back into the business of knocking on doors, urging like-minded citizens to register and vote.[51]

Republicans poured millions of dollars into ways of identifying, registering, and getting like-minded voters out to the polls. They were successful in 2002, by having a surge of Republican voters in key states like Florida, Missouri, Georgia, and North Carolina, and turning once competitive races into Republican victories. The 72-Hour Project was then ramped up for the 2004 presidential election. Thanks in great part to the 72-Hour Project, 10.5 million more Republicans voted in 2004 than in 2000. That effort was particularly important in the key battleground state of Ohio, where Republicans pulled off a victory for George W. Bush.

Democrats, too, had spent heavily in 2004, launching the most extensive and most expensive get-out-the-vote drive in American history. They did this by investing $135 million through their independent political organization, America Coming Together. Still, Democrats came up short, and were able to gain only 6.8 million new voters.[52] The trouble for Democrats was that they were simply out-hustled and out-organized by the veteran Republican team. Republican pollster Matthew Dowd estimated that using microtargeting and other research, the Bush campaign and the Republican National Committee were able to "quadruple the number" of Republican voters who could be targeted through direct mail, phone banks, and through door-to-door contact.[53]

But now with early voting through absentee ballots and mail-in votes, the 72-Hour Campaign, born just a few years ago, seems an anachronism. Now, there's no such thing as a 72-hour cycle. "It's 720 hours now," according to Rich Beeson, partner in the Republican voter contact firm FLS Connect and former political director of the Republican National Committee.[54] Further, notes Rob Jesmer, executive director of the National Republican Senatorial Committee, "classic GOTV" has gone from a week-long to a year-long process.[55] The congressional elections of 2010, with a building backlash of voter resistance to President Obama's agenda, saw intense mobilization, on all sides of the political aisle, well before election day.

7 Outside Voices

Contract killers out there in Super PAC land.
—Democratic consultant David Axelrod description of
Karl Rove (Crossroads GPS) and the Koch brothers
(Americans for Prosperity) (2012)

[We are] an organization of more than 2.2 million members united by
the belief in the dignity and worth of workers and the services they
provide and dedicated to improving the lives of workers and their families and creating a more just and humane society.
—Service Employees International Union (2010)

In the late 1980s and into the 1990s, American federal elections under-
went a competitive transformation. Congressional elections, usually
considered local contests focusing on local issues, became nationalized.
Probably the most concerted effort to nationalize these campaigns was the
1994 "Contract with America" drive of the Republican Party, with
Republican candidates throughout the country pledging to support a
common conservative policy agenda.

In other election cycles, it was the agenda of national interest groups that
came to the fore. No longer was it simply one candidate against another,
one campaign manager in a battle of wits against his counterpart. National
organizations stepped in to offer money, air issue ads, and provide logistical
support to get voters to the polls. National labor organizations, pro- and
anti-abortion forces, gun control and gun advocate organizations, and
groups supporting or opposing tort reform—these and many others now
felt a stake in local congressional races and tried to influence their outcomes.
In some cases, their efforts were coordinated with those of the candidates,
but in a number of instances, campaigns had little idea who was responsible
for the ads being aired or the money pouring into get-out-the-vote drives.

It became even more difficult when organizations or interests would
hide their true identity behind innocuous-sounding names, like
"Americans United for Justice," or "Protect Our Children Now." The

general public, and even at times the political consultants themselves, might never know whether the group behind a massive television advertising campaign represented twenty-five social justice organizations or the country's fifteen worst environmental polluters.

One early example of nationalization came in 1997. When California congressman Walter H. Capps died, a special election was held to fill the vacancy. Democrat Lois Capps, his wife, defeated Republican Tom Bordonaro in a tight, closely watched race. This special election wasn't simply about the qualifications of Capps and Bordonaro: it quickly became a battleground for pressing national social issues. The Campaign for Working Families, headed by conservative activist Gary Bauer, poured $200,000 into the campaign to portray Capps as pro-abortion. To counter that charge, the National Abortion Rights Action League spent $100,000, claiming that Bauer was an extremist. Joining the abortion issue was the policy debate over term limits. Capps said she favored term limits and was aided by $300,000 in media buys purchased by Americans for Term Limits and U.S. Term Limits. The television ads from national groups piled up, leaving Democratic political consultant Martin Hamburger to conclude that "voters were so terrorized by the torrent of issue advocacy campaigning going on that they paid attention to little or no advertising of any kind."[1]

We had entered into the era of political saturation of issue advocacy advertising in candidate campaigns. During the 2014 hotly contested Senate elections, outside money poured into campaigns. For example, in Kentucky (incumbent Mitch McConnell versus Democratic challenger Alison Lundergan Grimes), some $44.6 million was spent, with over $22.0 million coming from outside groups. In Colorado (incumbent Mark Udall versus Republican challenger Cory Gardner), a total of $37.5 million was spent, with over $27 million coming from outsiders.[2]

Every campaign manager tries to keep some control over the campaign. It is bad enough not knowing what the opponent will do, what news event might force a change in the campaign plan, or not know what one's own candidate might say. But with the nationalization of campaigns, it became far more difficult to manage, let alone control, campaign activity, given such uncertainty from all these new voices. The number and intensity of issue advocacy and other forms of campaign involvement by outside voices has only intensified during the past decade.

What Has Changed Over the Past Fifteen Years?

Online Political Activism

The creation of MoveOn.org in September 1998 marks a turning point in political activism. Wes Boyd and Joan Blades, frustrated by the attempt by congressional Republicans to impeach President Bill Clinton, created a website and an online petition, inviting their friends and like-minded citizens to pressure Congress to censure the president, not impeach him: "Censure President Clinton and Move On to Pressing Issues Facing the Nation." It was time, they thought, for the president to be rebuked, but then time to move on. Boyd and Blades, themselves Silicon Valley entrepreneurs, had struck a chord, and hundreds of thousands of people sought out their website, MoveOn.org, and thus began one of the first effective email activism campaigns. They tapped into a group of people who, until this time, had no unity and direction. MoveOn.org, using email communication, created a "flash campaign"—quickly sending out more than 250,000 telephone calls and more than 2 million emails to members of Congress urging them to vote against impeachment. Several wavering legislators acknowledged that the MoveOn campaign strengthened their resolve.

The unadorned MoveOn website had no graphics, no links to other sites, but had just a simple message: sign the petition, email it to others, and email it to your member of Congress. Through the MoveOn website, activists could control their message, raise campaign funds, and send out emails that would spiral out to millions of others. Immediately after the House voted for impeachment, an email from MoveOn was sent to its supporters, and by the next day $5 million had been pledged. A MoveOn political action committee was formed, and by mid-October 2000, it reported having $1.85 million in support for Democratic candidates, coming in from over 42,000 contributors. By 2001, MoveOn reported having 300,000 online activists; two years later, it had branched out to anti-war protest and other activities, and had 1.2 million supporters.[3]

In 2010, MoveOn boasted 5 million members, made up of MoveOn.org Civic Action, a 501(c)(4) nonprofit organization and MoveOn.org Political Action, a federal political action committee. The federal political action committee gave to progressive Democrats in the 2004 election cycle ($30 million), 2006 mid-term races ($28 million), 2008 election cycle ($38 million), and in its November 2010 FEC report, $25 million for the 2010 mid-term elections, coming from 6,033 contributors of $200 or more. By 2014, the amount MoveOn gave to candidates was just $10 million.[4]

As seen below, many other organizations have followed with online activism. The Tea Party movement, which started in 2009 with isolated protests that soon created a viral presence on the Internet, is in a way the mirror image of MoveOn: disaffected conservative, small government voices, who have strengthened and sustained themselves through both online and offline activism.

BCRA and the Emergence of 527 Organizations

During the late 1990s, and particularly with fundraising controversies surrounding the 1996 presidential election, it seemed as though every politician was in favor of campaign finance reform. Some of the reform ideas were far-reaching, but others had few teeth and were little more than window dressing. The one measure that finally became law was introduced by Senators John S. McCain (Republican-Arizona) and Russell Feingold (Democrat-Wisconsin). The McCain-Feingold legislation met stiff resistance in 1998, with a threatened Republican filibuster, but finally became law in 2002. After twenty-nine hearings, 522 witnesses, seventeen filibusters, and 113 votes on campaign fundraising reform in the decade preceding the vote, finally there was reform.[5]

McCain and Feingold were joined by Representatives Christopher Shays (Republican-Connecticut) and Martin Meehan (Democrat-Massachusetts) in sponsoring the Bipartisan Campaign Reform Act (BCRA), which finally became law in 2002. As noted in Chapter 4, one of the major reforms of BCRA was the ban on soft money and with that ban came the rediscovery of section 527 of the Internal Revenue Code. Section 527 had been around for decades, and was the part of the tax code used to set up tax-exempt organizations created to influence elections. Such organizations could not expressly advocate the defeat or the victory of a particular candidate, but they had wide latitude to become independent voices.

The 2004 presidential election was the first to see 527 organizations flex their muscle. Nearly $600 million was spent by these organizations. Given the extraordinary amount of money spent by 527 groups that year, it was safe to predict that 2008 would see even greater expenditures. But that was not the case. While outside groups were involved in all aspects of the campaign, during the 2008 presidential election, 527s spent roughly half of what they had spent four years earlier. One of the reasons for the diminished involvement, according to political scientist Stephen K. Medvic, was the uncertainty and ambiguous legal environment, both from Supreme Court rulings and from regulatory pronouncements from the Federal Election Commission.[6] Another reason was that both Obama and McCain discouraged their followers from collaborating in 527 independent action. But in the 2012 elections, 527s bounced back and during the early phases of the 2016 election, we see that 527s (along with Super PACs) will raise record amounts of money. Table 7.1 shows the largest 527 donors in 2004, 2008, and 2012 presidential election cycles.

The 527 and other organizations spent their millions of dollars to help candidates and causes in a variety of ways. America Coming Together, for example in 2004, the Democratic Party's outsourced 527, had the largest get-out-the-vote drive in U.S. history. MoveOn.org and many other 527s provided funds and in some cases manpower for get-out-the-vote efforts. Other organizations, like Swift Boat Veterans & POWs for Truth made their case through advocacy ads for or against presidential and other federal candidates.

Table 7.1 Largest 527 Donors, 2004, 2008, and 2012 Presidential Elections

2004	America Coming Together	$79,795,487 (pro-Kerry)
	Joint Victory Campaign 2004	$71,811,666 (pro-Kerry)
	Media Fund	$59,414,183 (pro-Kerry)
	Service Employees Intl. Union (SEIU)	$48,385,367 (pro-Kerry)
	Progress for America	$44,929,178 (pro-Bush)
	Swift Boat Veterans & POWs for Truth	$17,088,090 (anti-Kerry)
	MoveOn.org	$12,956,215 (anti-Bush)
	College Republican National Comm.	$12,780,126 (pro-Bush)
	New Democrat Network	$12,726,158 (anti-Bush)
	Club for Growth	$10,645,976 (pro-Bush)
2008	SEIU	$29,172,961 (pro-Obama)
	National Rifle Association	$6,944,377 (anti-Obama)
	National Republican Trust PAC	$6,592,924 (anti-Obama)
	MoveOn	$5,412,984 (pro-Obama)
	United Auto Workers	$4,860,569 (pro-Obama)
	SEIU Local 1199	$3,901,471 (pro-Obama)
	Let Freedom Ring	$3,361,707 (anti-Obama)
	American Issues Project	$2,878,872 (anti-Obama)
	Republican Majority Campaign	$2,519,640 (anti-Obama)
	AFSCME	$2,312,722 (anti-McCain)
2012	SEIU	$9,781,746 (Democratic)
	Plumbers/Pipefitters Union	$5,561,121 (Democratic)
	Intl. Brotherhood Electrical Workers (IBEW)	$5,483,343 (Democratic)
	Pharmaceutical Product Development	$5,058,150 (Republican)
	United Food & Commercial Workers	$3,837,328 (Democratic)
	Carpenters & Joiners Union	$3,464,810 (Democratic)
	Democratic Attorneys General Assn.	$2,210,000 (Democratic)
	AFSCME	$1,670,657 (Democratic)
	John Templeton Fdn.	$1,490,000 (Republican)
	DCCC	$1,462,656 (Democratic)

Source: OpenSecrets.org, "527 Committees: Top 50 Federally Focused Organizations," http://www.opensecrets.org/527s/527cmtes.php?level=C&cycle=2004; accessed August 15, 2009; "2010 Overview: 527 Committee Activity," http://www.opensecrets.org/overview/527cmtes.php; accessed August 15, 2009; Medvic, "Outside Voices," 199. 2012 data, from OpenSecrets.org, http://www.opensecrets.org/527s/527contribs.php?cycle=2012; accessed August 3, 2015.

In 2004, there were also a remarkable number of "fat cat" contributions from individual donors. About twenty-five individuals gave a total of $146 million to 527 groups, including George Soros ($23.4 million), Peter Lewis ($22.9 million), and Stephen Bing ($13.8 million), who each gave to progressive and liberal causes.[7] One of the key problems, however, was lack of coordination and consistent message between the 527 organizations and the Kerry campaign, which relied heavily on their assistance.

In 2010, the 527 organization generating the most money and energy was American Solutions for Winning the Future, a self-described "tri-partisan" citizens' action network made up of 1.5 million members, including 30,000 small businesses. That figure was somewhat disingenuous, because the bulk of the funds raised came from a handful of large energy-related and gaming industry-related corporations. American Solutions was founded by former Speaker of the House Newt Gingrich, and has raised over $28 million toward the 2010 mid-term elections, by far the largest amount raised by any 527 organization. But the bulk of the money raised went to pay for fundraising costs ($15 million), salaries ($3.8 million), and administration ($5 million), with just a couple of million left over for actual campaigning. One of its more vocal programs has been "Drill Here, Drill Now, Pay Less," an effort, despite the enormous 2010 BP oil spill off the Louisiana coast, to reduce American dependence on foreign sources of oil by drilling off America's coastal waters. Once Newt Gingrich became a presidential candidate, he left the organization, and it soon thereafter disbanded.[8]

In the 2008 congressional races, outside groups were particularly active. In the heated battle in North Carolina, pitting incumbent Republican senator Elizabeth Dole against Democratic challenger (and eventual winner) Kay Hagan, Dole was backed strongly by Freedom's Watch, which in ads in late October charged that Hagan supported increases in state and federal taxes. One ad had this line: "Kay Hagan voted for over 50 higher taxes and fees on income, birth, medical care, cars, food, even death." Not to be outdone, Hagan's campaign was aided by MoveOn.org which accused Dole of "being in the pocket of Big Oil," and the League of Conservation Voters (LCV), which added Dole to its list of "Dirty Dozen" legislators for her poor record on the environment.[9] (When Hagan was up for re-election in 2014, the outside money just poured into North Carolina. Altogether, $50.2 million was spent on the campaign, and of that amount, $37.6 million came from outside groups. Hagan was defeated.) In 2008 congressional races throughout the country, Freedom's Watch, a 501(c)(4) lobbying group planned to pour in $15 million into advertising and grassroots support to maintain Republican control of Congress and President Bush's policies, especially concerning the Iraq war.[10]

Probably the most significant outside help for Democrats running in 2008 congressional elections was the organizing efforts and enthusiasm spinning off the Obama campaign. In many districts, thousands of new Democratic voters were recruited for the first time, and directly aided the congressional Democratic candidates.

In the special election to fill the seat of the late Edward M. Kennedy, Democrats flooded Massachusetts with television ads, campaign flyers, and other communication to either support Martha Coakley or to attack Scott Brown: EMILY's List spent $250,000 on radio spots, the SEIU bought $700,000 in television advertising; the Democratic Senate Campaign Committee spent $567,000; the League of Conservation Voters spent $350,000 on television ads; MoveOn.org contributed $600,000; the National Democratic Party spent over $1 million. In all, Democratic groups and Coakley outspent Republicans and Brown by about two to one, along with a last-minute fly-in endorsement from President Obama.[11] Still, Brown prevailed.

Some 527 organizations were directed at specific races. In 2010, for example, Carly for California, mostly with funds coming from the candidate herself, was to assist Carly Fiorina in her bid to defeat Democratic senator Barbara Boxer. Arkansas for Change, an independent expenditure group composed of Arkansas labor unions, targeted Senator Blanche LIncoln. Didier for Senate assisted Clint Didier in his effort to win the Republican primary in Washington State. In all, approximately forty 527 groups filed financial disclosure reports for the 2010 mid-term. elections.[12]

During the heated 2014 congressional elections, 527 groups were particularly aggressive. What helped groups raise even more money was the lifting of the ceiling on how much an individual donor could give. The Supreme Court decision, *McCutcheon v. FEC*, decided in April 2014, lifted the contribution limits. Until this time, an individual could give a maximum of $123,200 over the course of a two-year election cycle; now, that cap was lifted. The Center for Responsive Politics found that just a tiny number, 591, of all contributors gave the maximum amount, but the potential was so much more for wealthy individuals intent on supporting candidates and political action committee.[13]

Table 7.2 Largest 527 Groups, 2014 Congressional Elections

Committee	Total Expenditures
ActBlue	$14,626,209
College Republicans	$14,156,096
SEIU	$10,872,872
EMILY's List	$ 9,894,653
Citizens United	$ 9,305,909
IBEW	$ 6,768,467
Gay, Lesbian Victory Fund	$ 7,175,540
Plumbers/Pipefitters Union	$ 5,796,679
RightChange.com	$ 5,206,186
GOPAC	$ 4,482,304

Source: Center for Responsive Politics

Millions were raised in the 2014 congressional races, giving a hint at the extraordinary amount of outside money that would be raised and spent in 2016.

Emergence of Forces on the Right—Tea Party

During the long recess in August 2009, members of Congress went back home to their districts and faced vocal and heated opposition to proposed national health care legislation that was under consideration. The anger of constituents went beyond health care, and burst forth into such areas as taxes, loss of jobs, the anemic economy, the bail-out of Wall Street financial firms, and a pent-up frustration with incumbent members of Congress. For many, this was their first exposure to what is now called the Tea Party movement. Later thousands of conservative protestors came to Washington, D.C., to voice their frustration. The march was organized by the 800,000 member Freedom Works (formerly Citizens for a Sound Economy), which was headed by former Texas congressman Richard K. Armey and Matt Kibbe.[14]

The Tea Party movement, formed in early 2009, is a legacy of protest movements begun decades ago, and most recently, from Ross Perot and his Reform Party movement in 1992 through Ron Paul's 2008 presidential bid. Paul dropped out of the Republican primary, gathering just 2 percent support, but he had ardent followers and was able to raise large amounts of money in single day rallies, called "money bombs." Like Paul's 2008 bid, the Tea Party movement, with its conservative, small government, libertarian impulses, has been aided by online technology in organizing followers and spreading its message.

In 2010, the Tea Party fielded or supported candidates in a number of Republican primaries, including successful bids in Kentucky, won by Rand Paul, the son of Ron Paul; in Nevada, where Sharron Angle defeated the mainstream Republican favorite in that state's primary; in Utah, where incumbent U.S. senator Robert Bennett was denied the Republican Party's nomination for another term. Scott Brown's special election victory was assisted by Tea Party voters, and Marco Rubio was handed the Republican nomination for the U.S. Senate in Florida when governor Charles Crist decided he could not win against Rubio and became an independent candidate instead. Ron Paul, Marco Rubio, Ted Cruz, and several other Tea Party-backed candidates were successful in the 2010, 2012, and 2014 general elections. Much of the anger and activism was lubricated by its online presence: social networking, email campaigns, websites, then channeled into grassroots, shoe-leather efforts. The Tea Party Patriots have their own television "network," hosted on its website with videos posted on YouTube. By 2014, the Tea Party movement had demonstrated that it was an important factor in Republican politics, winning some key races, but also losing some as well. The Republican establishment in the House of Representatives received a significant jolt when House majority leader Eric Cantor was defeated in a Virginia primary contest by a Tea Party-backed unknown, college professor Dave Brat, and when John Boehner was forced to retire in 2015.

Organizations of all ideological stripes participate in issue advocacy and advancing political candidates. EMILY's List and the National Abortion Rights Act League, organizations that are pro-choice, are countered by the Susan B. Anthony List, which promotes pro-life candidates for office. The whole panoply of interests attempt to influence the outcome of elections, from pro-gun control and anti-gun groups, tobacco, banking, insurance, casinos and gambling, oil and gas, pharmaceuticals, telephone utilities, health care professionals and companies, education, the entertainment industry, computer services, and many others.[15]

Post-Citizens United Activities

From 1907 through early 2010, corporations or labor unions could not give money directly to candidates. The U.S. Supreme Court's ruling in *Citizens United v. Federal Election Commission* kept intact the federal prohibition against direct corporate and union funding of candidates (it is done primarily through their political action committees), but now permits corporations to spend unlimited amounts of funds on direct advocacy for candidates for political office. This decision led to cries of foul from labor and progressive groups, and notably from Barack Obama during his 2010 State of the Union address. On the other hand, many Republican lawmakers and strategists, facing tough re-election fights in 2010, saw this January 2010 ruling as an opportunity to raise substantial amounts of corporate money on their behalf.

One of the first such organizations to emerge, calling itself an "action tank" (rather than a "think tank") is American Action Network. Former U.S. senator Norman B. Coleman, Jr. (Republican-Minnesota) headed this 501(c)(4) organization, and hoped to raise $25 million in support of about ten Republican Senate and twenty-five Republican congressional candidates. Peter H. Stone of the *National Journal* noted that there were about a dozen or so organizations, spanning the ideological spectrum, that were mounting multi-million dollar campaigns.[16] American Crossroads, another post-*Citizens United* organization, was launched by former White House political strategists Karl Rove and Ed Gillespie, with the intent of raising $60 million for Republican candidates.[17]

To counter the flow of cash from American Crossroads, the American Action Network, and other Republican-friendly campaign organizations, the AFL-CIO, American Federation of State, County, and Municipal Employees (AFSCME), and the Service Employees International Union (SEIU) raised and spent hundreds of millions of dollars. America Votes, a coalition of forty national organizations including the AFL-CIO and SEIU, spent $11.5 million to mobilize the progressive base, and Patriot Majority will spend $14 million in countering Tea Party candidates in about a dozen states.[18]

During the 2010 mid-term elections, all 435 congressional and thirty-seven Senate seats were contested. While the Republicans captured a record number of seats from the Democrats, the majority of the House seats were uncompetitive, with entrenched incumbents in safe seats. The focus for both parties was ninety House seats and a dozen Senate seats, and the high stakes of who would control Congress. A record $2 billion was poured into these races from the candidates themselves and outside organizations, for grassroots registration and get-out-the-vote drives, for issue advocacy ads and online communication.

By the 2014 congressional elections, even more outside money poured into Senate and key House races. As noted in Table 4.1, in many of the most expensive Senate races, outsiders spent more than the candidates themselves. In North Carolina, for example, outsiders spent well over twice the amount ($82.9 million) spent by the candidates ($37.8 million). In Alaska, outsiders likewise spent over twice ($41.4 million) the amount spent by candidates ($20.9 million). The same was true in Iowa, with outsiders spending $61.5 million, while the Senate candidates spend $29.6 million.

The *Citizens United* decision had no effect on campaign financial limit laws in place at the state and local level. However, the decision may have effectively overturned laws in twenty-four states that restricted or banned corporations for contributing to advocacy advertisement for or against state candidates.[19]

The nationalization of congressional elections, gaining traction in the 1980s, burst forth in campaigns during the first decade of the twenty-first century. The money pouring into such efforts has boosted the coffers of political consulting firms who specialize in polling, television and other old media advertising, new media communications, grassroots organization and get-out-the-vote drives. For example, in many hotly-contested 2014 congressional races, Super PACs, 501(c), 527s, and PACs invested heavily through independent expenditures. Thirty eight groups spent money on the California Seventh District race, twenty-eight outside groups spent independent money on the Colorado Sixth District, while twenty-eight groups spent independent money in the New Jersey Third District. In the Kentucky and Georgia Senate races, both contests were flooded with fifty-six outside groups trying to influence the elections. Some of the groups were long-standing participants in elections, like Sierra Club, the National Rifle Association, or the Service Employees International Union. Others were relatively new with ambiguous-sounding names, such as Protect America Today (conservative), Environment

America (liberal), American Unity PAC (conservative), or Patriot Majority USA (liberal).[20]

The competitiveness of the political parties, changeovers in party dominance in Congress during the decade, and the pressures from third party challenges have added to the nationalization trend. Add to this, the creation of 527 organizations, the aggressive fundraising of 501(c) organizations, the largesse of individual donors, and the determination of special interests to sway federal elections. Outside voices have had a major impact on determining the shape and character of federal elections over the past decade.

8 Campaigning in the Next Decade

Pity the poor political consultant, fundraisers, media strategists, pollsters and professional organizers. The ground is shifting under their feet and they are struggling in vain to maintain their balance.
—Karen A. B. Jagoda (2009)

The Internet isn't a line item in a campaign budget anymore. It's not just something you have to pay for, underneath catering and radio ads. It has reorganized the way Americans do everything—including electing their leaders. Candidates who would have had no chance before the Internet can now overcome huge odds, with the people they energize serving as the backbone of their campaign.
—Mindy Finn and Patrick Ruffini (2010)

Traditional politics is about centralized command and control. Internet politics, to be effective, needs to be about access and empowerment.
—Matthew R. Kerbel (2009)

Let us enjoy the familiar red and blue shadings while we can. They may not last much longer.
—Rhodes Cook (2007)

As we have seen in the previous chapters, there have been several profound changes in professional campaigning and campaign management over the past ten to fifteen years. However, the fundamental tasks for campaigns remain the same: how to effectively and efficiently communicate with the people who will vote for our candidate. Campaigns have to be able to reach young, college-aged online multi-taskers with the tools they are most familiar with and use all the time: text-messaging, social networks, smart phone applications, and websites. Campaigns likewise have to reach into nursing homes, where seniors gravitate to television, word of mouth, and newspapers. Failing to reach out to seniors, to college-aged voters, or to any other demographic can doom a campaign. And we have to remember that not every one is an activist; not all elections are exciting; and not every voter is young, hip and wired. Most voters are passive, still rely on television, and most elections are not life-changing, transformative events.

The Demographics of a Changing America

American society has been undergoing important, even fundamental demographic changes. As Gregory Spencer, chief of the U.S. Census Bureau's population projections branch, stated in 2004, "we've known for a long time that the U.S. is getting bigger, older, and more diverse." But we also know that Millennials, those born between 1982 and 2000, are now the biggest segment in America, representing more than one-quarter of the entire population. In data released by the Census Bureau in mid-2015, Millennials now number 83.1 million, exceeding the much-studied Baby Boomers (born between 1945 and 1960) who now number 75.4 million. Millennials are far more racially and ethnically diverse than Boomers.[1] With these changes come challenges that will ultimately be played out on Election Day.

The U.S. population was 151 million in 1950, went to 293 million by 2004, and is projected to reach 420 million by 2050. The Hispanic and Asian populations are expected to triple from 2000 to 2050. Hispanic population during this time span will increase from 36 million to 103 million, with their percentage in the population growing from 13 percent in 2000 to 24 percent in 2050. At the same time, the Non-Hispanic white population will grow more slowly and shrink to just 50 percent of the total population by 2050.

From the 1960s to the present, we have seen the once solidly Democratic South become heavily Republican and the once reliably Republican New England become steadfastly Democratic. We have also seen the Republican Party increasingly becoming the party of white voters, particularly older men. In the 2008 presidential election, parts of the red state South became even more red, while nine states that voted for Bush in 2004 were claimed by Obama. The success of the Republican Party and the Tea Party movement in the 2010 and 2014 mid-term elections underscores the restive mood of the country as it faces disillusionment, strains on the economy, and the activism of small-government, anti-government forces.

The demographic and social changes coming in the next decade and indeed in the next fifty years could be profound. As political analyst Rhodes Cook summarized it, "there is a blue-collar trend to the Republicans; a white-collar trend to the Democrats; an electorate that in the short run will be dominated by older voters, and in the long run dramatically impacted by a growing minority population."[2]

Table 8.1 U.S. Population in 2000 and Estimated in 2050 (in millions)

	2000	*2050*
Total Population	293	420
Hispanic	36 (13%)	103 (24%)
Non-Hispanic Whites	196 (69%)	210 (50%)
Black	36 (13%)	61 (15%)
Asian	11 (4%)	33 (8%)

Source: U.S. Census Bureau, "U.S. Interim Projections by Age, Sex, Race and Hispanic Origin." Available at http://www.census.gov/pc.www.usinterimproj; accessed August 15, 2009.

The Fundamentals of Campaigning

Looking ahead to the next decade, campaigning will look familiar, but there will be some important changes going on behind the scenes.

Survey Research

Landline telephone-based survey research will probably become just a niche market, overshadowed by online and automatic polling. This will happen both with public polls and most likely with private polls as well. Pollsters will have to devise ways to reach the growing number of persons who have only cell phones. Federal legislation may have to be changed to remove the bar from automatically calling cell phones; otherwise the price of manually placed calls makes them prohibitively expensive. Political consultant Mark Penn in 2010 predicted, "the next presidential election is probably the last presidential election where phone polling is the dominant methodology."[3] This was echoed by Jay Leve of SurveyUSA, a firm that does automated polls: "Today, nobody wants to get the phone." Polls, argues Leve, will be conducted on computer screen, appearing over in a corner, and respondents will reply at their leisure.[4] Yet pollster Paul Maslin, counters that the best way to reach a representative sample of the electorate is by "using paid interviewers, on the telephone, with the right questions prepared in a carefully crafted script, with the results used to plan campaign strategy—this will not go away."[5]

We should expect the number and frequency of media polls during presidential elections to remain high, and become even more ubiquitous with lower technology costs, expanding online pools of interviewees, and the flourishing of automated calls. Whether there is a corresponding increase in the frequency of statewide, down-ballot, and local issue public polling remains to be seen, and will probably depend more on the ability of local television and newspapers to pay for such surveys, their sense of civic obligation to their readers and viewers, and whether or not the candidates and issues are compelling enough to cover.

Fundraising

It took over twenty-five years to amend the basic federal campaign law, and once BCRA was in place, it was immediately challenged. BCRA has been upheld by the Supreme Court, but major portions of it have been modified, thanks to recent Supreme Court decisions. The 2010 decision *Citizens United* and subsequent rulings have made it far easier for big money to influence campaigns. Political action committee, corporate and labor advocacy Super PACs, 527 and 501(c)(4) campaign spending will most likely grow, particularly if the heated battles for partisan congressional dominance continue. As we have seen in the 2012 and now the 2016 presidential elections, Super PACs have become key outside players. They have kept some struggling candidates afloat, have poured millions into attack ads, have hired consultants and political operatives for get-out-the-vote and voter identification programs. To a large extent, Super PACs, with their innocuous-sounding names and their anonymous donors, have supplanted the political parties in presidential and some state-wide high-profile elections.

There will always be large-dollar individual donors; they are the bread and butter of most campaign fundraising. Intimate donor parties, big brassy fundraising bashes with a chance to have the donors' (and spouses') pictures taken with the candidate—these will always be part of the pageant of fundraising. Donors crave that connection, the sense of being considered an insider, and being thanked personally for helping out. No email thank you note will suffice.

The other fundraising trend will involve tapping into that enormous potential of small-dollar donors. Reaching into this market has always been the holy grail of fundraising. In pre-online days, it was immensely expensive (even counterproductive) to solicit funds from small-dollar donors. That has all changed with campaign websites and robust email messages linked to a video message and a "donate" button. Some campaigns now are trying to figure out how Twitter, with its 140-character line, can supplement the other online fundraising platforms.[6]

The potential, of course, is enormous. So few adults, less than 5 percent, ever contribute funds to political campaigns. If even 3 or 5 percent more can be reached, that could generate large sums of money. The problem, however, isn't technology: we've pretty well solved that problem. People are very accustomed to and feel secure in clicking a "donate" button on a trusted website or email message. The problem is one of civic engagement: citizens should not just talk about politics, register and vote, but reach into their pockets to assist candidates. If there are exciting candidates with compelling messages—like Barack Obama, Ted Cruz or Elizabeth Warren—their supporters will come and they will donate accordingly. But, frankly, most candidates for most elections are not that compelling, that interesting, or their messages are not that powerful.

Voter Information

Without a doubt, the next decade will bring campaigns more and more accurate information about where people live, how they vote, what their lifestyle choices are, what they watch on television, what they search for online, and what habits they indulge in. As one newspaper headline aptly put it, "The GOP Knows You Don't Like Anchovies."[7] The science (and art) of micro-targeting will probably reach more sophisticated levels in the decade to come. Data management companies are increasing their information, pooling data sources, constantly updating files, and making much more sophisticated analyses than before. The old assumptions of reliable Republican or dependable Democratic segments of the voting population will be challenged, as the parties and candidates try to peel off voters and identify new supporters.

Online Communication

It is exciting to think what magic lies ahead when imagining the tools for online communication. In 2025, might we look back at the fanciest of laptops, tablets, and the sleekest cell phone of today and see how clunky, slow moving, weak on memory, and expensive they were. Will we reach that grand convergence that futurists and technologists have been predicting for years? Are we in the twilight years of the "old media," in the maturing years of the "new media," but about to step into simply "media"? Did the communications originate as a television video, a web video, a radio segment, a podcast, a magazine article, or a software game? It doesn't matter, because it all ends up seemlessly streamed—converged—onto our tablets, smart phones, watch computers, or some other media platform. It might be a 65-inch 4K Ultra HD, 3D television screen, that 2.5-by-4 inch inch cell phone monitor, or the 8-by-10 inch tablet computer. All media become one. We aren't there yet, but certainly the day will come.

In the next decade we also might be confronted with new cognitive patterns. In 2010, the Pew Research Center found that half of American teenagers (12 through 17), send an average of fifty and more text and instant messages a day, and that one-third of American teenagers send more than 100 such messages a day. Two-thirds of teens said they would use their cell phones to text friends rather than call them. The Kaiser

Family Foundation in 2010 found that Americans, ages eight through eighteen, spend an average of seven and one-half hours a day using some form of electronic device.[8]

The digital age has made so many of us multi-taskers: talk on the cell phone, watch a streaming video, eat lunch, and surf through our email, all at once. In doing all this, we are trying to be more efficient, and can do so, because our brains aren't being asked to process difficult or complicated tasks. But, according to digital information expert Linda Stone, many people today live in *continuous partial attention*. This is not multi-tasking, but rather paying partial attention continuously. "We pay continuous partial attention in an effort not to miss anything," Stone argues. "It is an always-on, anywhere, anytime, any place behavior that involves an artificial sense of constant crisis. We are always on high alert when we pay continuous partial attention." But in being so accessible, we become inaccessible. "The latest, greatest powerful technologies have contributed to our feeling increasingly powerless." As we become more enamored of the seemingly limitless information available, it may become even harder for candidates and campaigns to grab the attention and focus of the truly determinedly wired.[9]

Down-Ballot Campaigns, Old and New Techniques

Much of the discussion in this book has focused on the wizardry of new online communication tools and technological improvements to the campaign process. The discussion has also centered heavily on presidential elections, where these changes are most evident. Yet, even with all the new emphasis on online contributions and new marketing techniques employed in recent elections, the great majority of money raised was plowed back into the traditional sources of campaign expenditures: television advertising, persuasion direct mail, telephone calls, staff and consultants. As Michael Cornfield and Lee Rainie remind us, "twenty-first-century fundraising is paying for the same old-fashioned communications mechanisms that have dominated U.S. politics since the 1960s."[10]

Yet, the vast majority of elections are down ballot and local: small town mayor, sheriff, members of the state general assembly, or ballot issues concerning local matters. And it is at this level perhaps more than any other area, where the twentieth century methods of communication still are key: the face-to-face meetings with candidates, door-to-door canvassing, volunteer phone banks, yard signs, bumper stickers, and direct mail literature. Nevertheless, candidates at the very local level also discover the advantages of building email lists of followers, developing simple but effective websites, buying voter contact information, creating social networking pages, and sending messages through Twitter accounts. All are relatively inexpensive, smart ways of communicating.

Political Consulting and Campaigns

For the last several years, the e-Voter Institute has surveyed consultants and advocacy leaders and voters who are comfortable with using online communication. What the Institute has discovered is a disconnection between what the voters want and what consultants say is effective. Karen A. B. Jagoda, president and co-founder of the e-Voter Institute, observed that "consultants are missing some of the signs from voters about how to break through the media clutter in their lives." Looking at its 2008 survey results, Jagoda asserted that "political consultants underestimated the value" of candidate websites, online ads, webcasts, and "perhaps over-estimate the value of email."[11] Surely after the lessons from the 2008 and 2012 presidential campaigns, consultants and candidates are rethinking the importance of such online tools to reach voters and learning to integrate them.

Mindy Finn, Republican online campaign consultant who worked for the Mitt Romney 2008 campaign, and her business partner Patrick Ruffini wrote in early 2010:

> We've been working to get the GOP into the Web era for the past decade. We've been laughed out of high-level campaign meetings, told that online budgets are the first thing to go and informed that having a Facebook page is "unpresidential." And it wasn't until recently that people stopped asking us to fix their computers.[12]

Successful campaigns of the future will recognize the need for a complete integration of all aspects of communication, including micro-targeting analysis. There will be a communications team, not separate old media and new media communications teams. They will be fully coordinated and online staffers will be fully integrated into the strategic decision-making.

Republicans had a wake up call in the 2008 elections. By 2010, nearly 89 percent of Republican members of Congress had their own YouTube channels, while 74 percent of Democratic members had channels. Eight out of the top ten such viewed channels on YouTube came from Republican members of Congress.[13] Symbolically, if nothing else, John McCain in 2008 was probably the last of the twentieth century campaigners. (Ironically, McCain's 2000 presidential campaign has been viewed as one of the early milestones in online campaigning.) He famously did not use (or know how to use) email. But by the time of his tight re-election campaign to the Senate in 2010, McCain himself was a convert. He had a Twitter account, and was enthusiastically tweeting away on a regular basis.[14] The 2012 Romney presidential campaign was fully engaged in technological tools, microtargeting techniques, social media, and online communication. Yet it still came up short in comparison to the technology-driven Obama re-election campaign.

With all the changes in campaign technology, social media, and the like, are political consultants and political operatives obsolete? Are they relics of twentieth century ways of electing candidates to office? The answer, I believe, is clearly no. Political consultants—from campaign managers, specialists in communications, research, outreach and voter contact, and all the rest—will continue to play a vital role in elections at all levels. In fact, the role of the top strategy team is even more important as we become more of a wired, informed, and perhaps chaotic society. With messages and slogans, information and misinformation flying in all directions, it is vital to establish control and bring some semblance of order. Often characterized as "hired guns" or worse, political consultants play an important role in helping candidates wade through the formidable obstacles to get their message across and present themselves before voters. As political scientist David Dulio asserts, "professional political consultants are not the bane of the U.S. electoral system. In fact, their appearance and increased presence in elections can benefit democracy."[15]

The campaigning of 2025 will undoubtedly call for sharper skills and greater ability of the consulting team to lead, set strategy, but also to engage voters so that their enthusiasm and their drive complements the efforts of the campaign.

Three Paths

With this continuing revolution in digital technology and communication, we might see three distinct paths lying ahead of us in the next decade.

The Engaged, Digital Citizenry

Thanks to online communication, citizens could become far more engaged, more interested in the public sphere, more concerned about who represents them, more active in thinking about the public good, public policy, and improving their lot in life and the lives of others. They could be surrogates for candidates, using their own enthusiasm and energy to talk to strangers and neighbors, help finance campaigns, and carry on the truly fundamental aspects of democratic affairs. Political campaigns can encourage citizen participation and shed the attitude that only top-down command and control works. Instead of treating a campaign as though it is no place for amateurs, political consultants could encourage citizen participation, help guide it, energize it, and use it as a compelling force in their campaigns. The key, argues online communications expert Julie

Barko Germany, is that "campaigns have to engage people, not push them."[16]

The Angry, Disillusioned Online Activist

We could become a nation further pulled apart, with a growing gap in our wealth, stress from the further loss of manufacturing and our place in the world's markets, a nation tugged apart by cries for separation, a growing cultural and intellectual divide, and the urging of simplistic solutions to complex problems. This could lead to further bursts of anger and disillusionment with the whole system of government, loss of trust in elected officials—no matter their partisan or ideological stripe, and impassioned pleas for returning us to a time that never was, but for which we yearn. Online communication is a perfect platform for the angry and embittered, for hatred and prejudice. As we have witnessed in the 2016 presidential primaries, candidates have and will undoubtedly continue to tap into this frustration and anger.

The Citizen Feeding on Fantasy

Or we may become a country soft in luxuries, mesmerized by the far more interesting entertainment and fantasies that make us HD, 3D television-watching zombies, far more wrapped up in sports, celebrities, and music videos than the boring pseudo-realities of campaigning and elections. People are numbed, content, and simply not interested in voting and participation in the public sphere. The wonder of the great convergence, with its 500 channels, is that it is so wonderful, so mesmerizing, that, in Neil Postman's apt phrase, we are "amusing ourselves to death."[17] The response from political campaigns could be equally pernicious: fluff and nonsense, symbols rather than substance. We are already there to a much greater measure than we would like to admit.

All three of these impulses—the engaged, the angry, and the tuned-out—are very much present in today's communication and civic culture. They are fueled and stoked by the money pumped in by Super PACs and other third parties, by viral communication, and by the buzz of social media.

As we see in the 2016 presidential election, and as we have seen in the 2014 congressional elections, there is plenty of frustration and anger to go around. The interesting dynamic will be between the engaged voter and the tuned out. Voter participation rates were low during the 2014 elections, often meaning that just those engaged and passionate enough were eager to cast their votes. The majority of voters sat on the sidelines. During the 2015 pre-primary season and during the primaries themselves, we have seen the depths of anger and frustration among voters, and the ideological rifts in both the Republican and Democratic parties. We also have the unusual feature of dynastic candidates (Bush and Clinton) versus self-proclaimed outsiders (Trump, Sanders, Carson, Fiorina, and others). As the Republicans and Democrats make their choices and ultimately face off in the 2016 general election, we can only hope that the engaged, active citizen, seeking to improve the public good will prevail. And that in our age of pervasive media attention, viral communications, and big money, that model of engaged and enlightened citizenry will carry us into the next decade of politics and campaigning.

Appendix A
Summary of Findings

The Modern Campaign

1. The twentieth century model of professional campaigning, emphasizing top-down decision-making, dominated by television has been replaced by a twenty-first century model with online communication, greater use of technology, more sense of citizen involvement, opportunities for small donor giving, well-financed outside forces, and reliance on research and metrics.

Communicating with Voters: The New Media

2. We now live in a wired world, with a large majority of citizens who use online communications and expect their politicians and candidates to communicate through such means.
3. New technologies and online communication—particularly campaign websites, YouTube and web videos, email, mobile phones, political blogs, and social networking sites—have fundamentally altered the relationship between candidates and voters, and among voters themselves.
4. Online advertising is just beginning to realize its potential.
5. Thanks to online communication, there is a far greater volume of information available to voters.
6. More than ever, campaign communications are now instantaneous.
7. Online communication opens up campaigns to rumor, innuendo, with no waiting for the facts.
8. Candidates can now easily be caught off-guard with the ever present camera, and the web video capabilities of YouTube and other sites.
9. Most importantly, online campaigns can become open-sourced and engage citizens to a far greater extent.

Communicating with Voters: The Old Media

10. Americans turn to television as their main source of information, but there has been a steady decline as viewers turn to alternative sources.
11. There is a further fragmentation of the audience.

12. For political (and all) advertisers, digital video recorders that can block out ads are becoming a growing concern.
13. There has been a substantial increase in presidential-year television advertising, but in selected battleground markets only.
14. Candidates have had to resort to inventive ways of obtaining free media.
15. There has been an increase in negative campaigning at the federal level.
16. Campaigns have been turning more to branding and framing techniques.
17. There is an increase in "faux television."
18. The *Citizens United* decision has opened the floodgates for independent expenditures, from 501(c) groups and Super PACs in particular.
19. Campaign commercials have relied on focus group, dial testing, and mall testing techniques to assure that they are tuned into viewers' responses.
20. There is a new breed of videographer, shooting *cinéma vérité* style, often for web videos.
21. Direct mail has been transformed by the technologies of the craft and by microtargeting. New technologies allow cable television to microtarget their subscribers viewing habits.
22. Online communication is active; watching television is passive, and this makes an important difference in campaign communicating.

Campaign Dollars

23. The cost of campaigns at the federal level (presidential, Senate and House) has risen dramatically, even adjusted for inflation. Some of the biggest increases have come in California ballot initiative issues. In many local contests, campaigns remain relatively low cost, while in others, they have jumped tremendously.
24. Federal campaign law was changed in significant ways by BCRA in 2002, but then altered radically by Supreme Court and other federal court decisions in subsequent years.
25. The Supreme Court, by permitting unlimited corporate and union spending for advocacy advertising, has dramatically changed the landscape of federal campaign law.
26. The way that campaigns solicit and receive funds has changed dramatically. Bundling has increased; online contributions now form a significant part of the contribution base, but still fall short of mega-donations.
27. There has been some increase in the percentage of voters who donate to political campaigns (not including through income tax check offs), but the percentage is still quite low.
28. Thanks to *Citizens United* and other cases, we are now in the era of dark money, non-reportable funds, with no limits placed upon them. This is fundamentally changing the nature of campaign financing.

Taking the Pulse of the Electorate

29. There is more polling than ever at the presidential level.
30. There is a shrinking response rate.
31. Voter lists are replacing random digit dialing.
32. Survey researchers continue to struggle with how to capture the views of cell phone-only respondents.
33. Internet polling is making great strides in acceptance during the 2000s, but some political consultants remain skeptical.
34. Robocall polls are becoming more and more prevalent in media outlets, but still suspect by others.
35. Brushfire polls are also appearing; with the main attraction being their price and quick turnaround.
36. Thanks to online sources, nearly anyone can become a pollster and ask those questions.

Voter Identification, Contact, and Mobilization

37. There is better access to voter registration information.
38. Microtargeting techniques have been greatly improved and used widely to identify probable supporters.
39. There have been important advances in voter contact through emailing, text messaging, and smart phone applications.
40. Campaigns have been impacted by the trend to early voting.
41. There has been a growing use of robocalls and push-polling in campaigns.
42. The 72-hour campaign has been created, but now challenged by early voting.

Outside Voices

43. Online political activism, beginning in the late 1990s, becomes an important component of campaigns and elections.
44. Emergence of 527 organizations, and further emergence of 501(c) groups, and later Super PACs as important voices in advocacy.
45. Emergence of online/offline forces on the Right, especially the Tea Party activists.
46. Growing corporate, labor, and big money involvement since *Citizens United*.

Appendix B

Timeline of Selected Campaign Firsts

1995 Lamar Alexander is first presidential candidate to announce his candidacy over the Internet.

1996 Bob Dole announces his campaign website address during the first presidential debate (October).

1997 Ted Mondale, candidate for governor in Minnesota, is first candidate to buy political advertising on a political website (October).

1998 Reform Party candidate, Jesse Ventura, credits the Internet with helping him organize volunteers, raise money, and control the flow of information.
Creation of MoveOn.org in response to attempt to impeach President Clinton.

1999 Arizona becomes first state to allow online voting in its presidential primary.

2000 Republican presidential hopeful, Senator John McCain of Arizona, raises over half a million dollars online in just one day, and over $2 million online in one week (March).
Presidential nominating conventions were webcast for the first time.
First presidential campaign when online surveys are used.

2002 Passage of the Bipartisan Campaign Finance Reform Act (BCRA) (November).
Republicans inaugurate the 72-hour campaign.

2003 Democratic presidential hopeful, former Vermont governor Howard Dean, becomes first major party candidate to post a blogsite (March).

Internet is used in an effort to draft former general Wesley Clark for president (April).

Dale Dougherty of O'Reilly Media coined the term "Web 2.0."

2004   Democratic nominee John Kerry announces John Edwards as his running mate through an email; about 150,000 email addresses are collected by the Kerry campaign in anticipation of that announcement.

527 political organizations (such as Americans Coming Together, Media Fund, Progress for America, Swift Boat Veterans for Truth) become important voices in U.S. presidential elections.

2005   YouTube created (February); bought by Google in November 2006.

2006   Twitter goes public (March).

2007   Hillary Clinton announces her presidential ambitions on her website, declaring "I'm In to Win" (January).

2008   Presidential candidates Barack Obama and Hillary Clinton compete throughout entire calendar of Democratic primaries. Obama campaign smashes all records for fundraising, much of it coming from online, small donor sources.

Twenty-eight states permit some form of early voting.

2009   San Francisco mayor Gavin Newsom announces his candidacy for governor of California on Twitter and Facebook (April).

2010   Supreme Court rules, in *Citizens United v. FEC*, that corporations and labor unions can spend unlimited funds for express advocacy campaigns in federal campaigns (January).

Tim Pawlenty crowdsources his fundraising; giving supporters a say in who should receive campaign funds.

2011   Obama re-election campaign begins in earnest, with eventual investment of a hundred million dollars in campaign technology. Big-time contributors, like Sheldon Adelson and the Koch brothers, donate millions to assist Republican candidates and to try to defeat Obama. In all, the Koch brothers spent $407 million.

2012   The presidential contest between Obama and Romney becomes the most expensive in history.

Obama campaign employs tool called "Optimizer" to help finely tune cable television messages. Romney campaign introduces Project Orca while Obama campaign employs Project Narwhal.

2014   Republicans redouble efforts to gain control of the U.S. Senate and increase control over the House of Representatives. Greatly aided by conservative Super PAC money.

2015   Four Democrats take on Hillary Clinton for the Democratic Party's nomination, while seventeen Republicans vie for their nomination. Jeb Bush, Ted Cruz, and some several Super PACs raise enormous amounts of money.

Notes

Preface

1 "The First Clinton-Dole Presidential Debate," October 6, 1996, Debate Transcript. Commission on Presidential Debates website, http://www.debates.org/pages/trans96a.html, accessed August 15, 2009.

1 The Modern Campaign

Epigraph quotes from Garrett M. Graff, "Barack Obama: How Content Management and Web 2.0 Helped Win the White House," *Infonomics*, March–April 2009; AIIM website, http://www.aiim.org/Infonomics/Obama-How-Web2.0-Helped-Win-Whitehouse.aspx; accessed May 28, 2010; Sophia Yan, "How Scott Brown's Social-Media Juggernaut Won Massachusetts," *Time*, February 4, 2010; and Robert Costa, Laura Vozzella, and David A. Fahrenthold, "Republican House Majority Leader Eric Cantor Succumbs to Tea Party Challenger Dave Brat," *Washington Post*, June 11, 2014.

1 Paul S. Herrnson, "The Evolution of Political Campaigns," in Paul S. Herrnson, ed., *Guide to Political Campaigns in America* (Washington, D.C.: CQ Press, 2005), 19–36. Dennis W. Johnson, "Amateur Hour: American Political Consultants and Citizen Activism," unpublished paper presented at the Fifty-second Annual Meeting of the British Association of American Studies, University of Leicester, April 20, 2007.

2 For a summary of the political science literature on campaigning and the Internet, see Dennis W. Johnson, "Campaigning and the Internet," in Stephen C. Craig, ed., *The Electoral Challenge: Theory Meets Practice* (Washington, D.C.: CQ Press, 2006), 121–142; Kristen Foot and Stephen Schneider, *Web Campaigning* (Cambridge: MIT Press, 2006); and Bruce Bimber and Richard Davis, *Campaigning Online: The Internet in U.S. Elections* (New York: Oxford University Press, 2003).

3 Bimber and Davis, *Campaigning Online*.

4 For analysis of the 2004 presidential campaign and Dean's campaign in particular, see Andrew Paul Williams and John C. Tedesco, eds., *The Internet Election: Perspectives on the Web in Campaign 2004* (Lanham, Md.: Rowman & Littlefield, 2006); Daniel Kreiss, *Taking Our Country Back? Political Consultants and the Crafting of Networked Politics From Howard Dean to Barack Obama*, unpublished Ph.D. dissertation, Stanford University, 2010; and

insider accounts by Joe Trippi, *The Revolution Will Not Be Televised: Democracy, the Internet, and the Overthrow of Everything* (New York: Regan Books, 2004), and Zephyr Teachout and Tom Streeter, eds., *Mousepads, Shoe Leather, and Hope* (Boulder: Paradigm Publishers, 2008).

5 Quoted in Jerome Armstrong and Marko Moulitsas Zuniga, *Crashing the Gate: Netroots, Grassroots, and the Rise of People-Powered Politics* (White River Junction, Vt.: Chelsea Green Publishing, 2006), 96.

6 David Plouffe, *The Audacity to Win: The Insider Story and Lessons of Barack Obama's Historic Victory* (New York: Vikin, 2009), 237.

7 Graff, "Barack Obama: How Content Management and Web 2.0 Helped Win the White House."

8 Ibid., 38.

9 Ibid.

10 Ibid.

11 Yan, "How Scott Brown's Social-Media Juggernaut Won Massachusetts."

2 Communicating with Voters: The New Media

Epigraph on Newsom in Carla Marinucci, "Newsom Makes His Official Governor Bid Online," *San Francisco Chronicle*, April 21, 2009; Jennifer Steinhauer, "Dose of Venom for Candidates Turns Ads Viral," *New York Times*, March 21, 2010, A1; and Ted Cruz twitter, @TedCruz (March 23, 2015).

1 See Dennis W. Johnson, "Campaigning on the Internet," in Stephen C. Craig, ed., *The Electoral Challenge: Theory Meets Practice* (Washington, D.C.: CQ Books, 2006), Appendix: Selected Internet Campaign Milestones, 139–141.

2 "Internet User Demographics," Pew Research Center on Internet, Science and Technology, January 2014, http://www.pewinternet.org/data-trend/internet-use/latest-stats/; accessed June 22, 2015.

3 Aaron Smith, "U.S. Smartphone Use in 2015," Pew Research Center, April 1, 2015, http://mobilestatistics.com/mobile-devices/, accessed June 22, 2015.

4 "Internet's Broader Role in Campaign 2008," Pew Research Center for the People & the Press, January 11, 2008, http://people-press.org/report/384/internets-broader-role-in-campaign-2008; accessed August 15, 2009.

5 Ibid. and "In the Changing New Landscape, Even Television Is Vulnerable," Pew Research Center, September 27, 2012, http://www.people-press.org/2012/09/27/in-changing-news-landscape-even-television-is-vulnerable/; accessed June 23, 2015.

6 "Persuading and Motivating Voters: What Will It Take in 2010?" e-Voter Institute, October 2009. Karen A. B. Jagoda of e-Voter Institute, Rich Berke, Kendall Anderson, Michelle Lamberty, and Young Ju Yoon of HCD conducted the research. N=1,476.

7 Bruce Bimber and Richard Davis, *Campaigning Online: The Internet in U.S. Elections* (New York: Oxford University Press, 2003), Chapter 2, and Steven M. Schneider and Kirsten A. Foot, "Web Campaigning by U.S. Presidential Primary Candidates in 2000 and 2004," in *The Internet Election* edited by Williams and Tedesco, 21. For a survey of the academic literature on elections and the Internet, see Johnson, "Campaigning on the Internet,".

8 Bimber and Davis, *Campaigning Online*, 165–171.

9 Schneider and Foot, "Web Campaigning by U.S. Presidential Primary Candidates in 2000 and 2004," 25–30.

10 Ibid., 28–30.

11 On the Dean online campaign, see Daniel Kreiss, "Taking Our Country Back?: Political Consultants and the Crafting of Networked Politics from Howard Dean to Barack Obama," unpublished Ph.D. dissertation, Stanford University, June 2010.

12 "YouTube Serves Up 100 Million Videos a Day Online," USA Today, July 16, 2006; http://www.usatoday.com/tech/news/2006-07-16-youtubeviews_x. htm?; accessed June 14, 2010.

13 Stephen E. Frantzich, "E-Politics and the 2008 Presidential Campaign," in William J. Crotty, ed., *Winning the Presidency 2008* (Boulder: Paradigm Publishers, 2009), 147.

14 From the transcripts of the Democratic debate, http://www.cnn.com/2007/ POLITICS/07/23/debate.transcript/index.html; http://www.cnn.com/2007/ POLITICS/07/23/debate.transcript.part2/index.html; Republican debate: http://www.cnn.com/2007/POLITICS/11/28/debate.transcript/index. html; http://www.cnn.com/2007/POLITICS/11/28/debate.transcript.part2/ index.html; accessed June 12, 2010.

15 From the UStream website, http://www.mikegravel.us/content/mikes-alternative-debate-live-tonight-january-3; accessed June 9, 2010.

16 Michael Cornfield, *Politics Moves Online: Campaigning and the Internet* (New York: Century Foundation, 2004), 27.

17 Bimber and Davis, *Campaigning Online*, 53.

18 *The Politics-To-Go Handbook: A Guide on Using Mobile Technology in Politics* (Washington, D.C.: George Washington University, Institute on Politics, Democracy and the Internet, 2005).

19 Twitter, "Where Does Twitter Come From? About Twitter," from http:// twitter.com.about; accessed January 3, 2010. Also, Danah M. Boyd and Nicole B. Ellison, "Social Networking Sites: Definition, History, and Scholarship," *Journal of Computer-Mediated Communication* 13 (1) (October 2007): 210–230; and Lee Humphreys, "Mobile Social Networks and Social Practice: A Case Study of Dodgeball," *Journal of Computer-Mediated Communication* 13 (1) (October 2007): 341–360.

20 Mindy Finn, "What Wins A Vote?" *Politics* (January 2010), 74.

21 "Is the Key to Number 10 a High Social Standing?" *Marketing Week*, April 22, 2010; http://www.marketingweek.co.uk/in-depth-analysis/coverstories/ is-the-key-to-number-10-a-high-social-standing?/3011937article; accessed April 22, 2010.

22 Antoinette Pole, *Blogging the Political: Politics and Participation in a Networked Society* (New York: Routledge, 2010), 113. See also, Eric Boehlert, *Bloggers on the Bus: How the Internet Changed Politics and the Press* (New York: Free Press, 2009).

23 Joseph Graf, "The Audience for Political Blogs: New Research on Blog Readership," George Washington University Institute for Politics, Democracy and the Internet, October 2006.

24 Kevin A. Pirch, "Bloggers at the Gate: Ned Lamont, Blogs, and the Rise of Insurgent Candidates," in Costas Panagopoulos, ed., *Politicking Online: The*

Transformation of Election Campaign Communications (New Brunswick: Rutgers University Press, 2009), 217–232.

25 On the 2004 election and blogging, see Kaye D. Trammell, "The Blogging of the President," in *The Internet Election*, edited by Williams and Tedesco, 133–146.

26 On the Dean online activities, see Kreiss, "Taking Our Country Back?"

27 Jose Antonio Vargas, "Grass Roots Planted in Cyberspace," *Washington Post*, March 30, 2007, C1.

28 Jose Antonio Vargas, "Obama's Wide Web," *Washington Post*, August 20, 2008; Howard Fineman, "What Have We Created?" *Newsweek*, November 3, 2008, 54; Jose Antonio Vargas, "Obama Raised Half a Billion Online," *Washington Post*, November 20, 2008.

29 David Talbot, "How Obama *Really* Did It," *Technology Review*, September–October 2008, 79.

30 Julie Germany, "Advances in Campaign Technology," in Dennis W. Johnson, ed., *Campaigning for President 2012: Strategy and Tactics* (New York: Routledge, 2013), 82; Lauren Duggan, "Social Media Then and Now: The 2008 and 2012 Presidential Elections," Media Bistro, January 31, 2012, http://www.mediabistro.com/alltwitter/social-media-then-and-now-the-2008-and-2012-presidential-elections-infographic_b18132; accessed June 2, 2015.

31 Karen Jagoda and Nick Nyhan, "E-Voter 98: Measuring the Impact of Online Advertising for a Political Candidate: A Case Study," 2d ed. (Westhill Partners, January 1999), http://evoterinstitute.com/wp-content/uploads/2009/03/evoter98report.pdf; accessed June 23, 2015.

32 Michael Cornfield and Kate Kaye, "Online Political Advertising: The Prehistoric Era Continues," 720 Strategies, http://www.720strategies.com/site/page/online_political_advertising_the_prehistoric_era_continues; accessed June 1, 2010. See also, Lynda Lee Kaid, "Political Web Wars: The Use of the Internet for Political Advertising," in *The Internet Election* edited by Williams and Tedesco, 67–82.

33 Cornfield and Kaye, "Online Political Advertising."

34 Kate Kaye, "Google Grabbed Most of Obama's $16 Million in 2008," ClickZ website, January 6, 2009, http://www.clickz.com/3632263.

35 Chris Anderson, *The Long Tail: Why The Future of Business is Selling Less of More* (New York: Hyperion, 2006); Josh Koster, "Long-Tail Nanotargeting," Politics, February 2009, http://www.politicsmagazine.com/magazine-issues/february-2009/long-tail-nanotargeting/; accessed May 28, 2010.

36 Kate Kaye, "GOP Outguns Dems Online in Congressional Races," ClickZ website, April 21, 2010, http://www.clickZ/3640136; accessed May 28, 2010.

37 Nick Judd, "In Online Political Ads, Facebook is Catching Up to Google," TechPresident Personal Democracy Forum, May 24, 2010, http://techpresident.com/blog-entry/online-political-ads-facebook-catching-google; accessed May 28, 2010.

38 Alex Fitzpatrick, "2012 Is the Year of the Online Political Ad," Mashable, May 1, 2012, http://mashable.com/2012/05/01/year-political-ad; accessed June 30, 2015, cited in Germany, "Advances in Campaign Technology," 85.

39 Germany, "Advances in Campaign Technology," 86–87.

40 Jeffrey B. Abramson, F. Christopher Arterton, and Gary R. Orren, *The Electronic Commonwealth: The Impact of New Technologies on Democratic Politics* (New York: Basic Books, 1988), 4–5, 32–65.

41 Alan Rosenblatt, "Dimensions of Campaigns in the Age of Digital Networks," in James A. Thurber and Candice J. Nelson, *Campaigns and Elections American Style*, Fourth edition (Boulder: Westview Press, 2014), 175–96, at 179–80.

42 Michael X. Delli Carpini, "Voters, Candidates, and Campaigns in the Information Age: An Overview and Assessment," *The Harvard International Journal of Press/Politics* 1 (4) (Fall, 1996), 37.

43 Lee Rainie, Michael Cornfield, and John Horrigan, *The Internet and Campaign 2004* (Washington, D.C.: Pew Internet & American Life Project and Pew Research Center for the People and the Press, March 6, 2005). Available at http://www.pewinternet.org; excerpted in Clifford A. Jones, "Campaign Finance Reform and the Internet: Regulating Web Messages in the 2004 Election and Beyond," in *The Internet Election*, edited by Williams and Tedesco, 6.

44 McCurry quoted in Jon Fine, "Election 2008: Blogs, Schmogs!" *Businessweek*, September 29, 2008, 85.

45 Andrew Rasiej and Micah Sifry, "The Web: 2008's Winning Ticket," *Politico*, November 12, 2008.

46 Fred Aun, "Over Long Campaign, Obama Videos Drew Nearly a Billion Views," ClickZ, November 7, 2008; http://clickz.com/3631604; accessed May 28, 2010.

47 DrudgeReport.com, accessed July 1, 2015.

48 DiFonzo quoted in Bob Secter, "Political Rumors, Full of Sound and Fury, Fly Fast Online," *Chicago Tribune*, October 17, 2008.

49 Nicholas DiFonzo, "Political Rumors in the 2008 Election," *Psychology Today*, October 29, 2008; http://psychologytoday.com/blog/around-the watercooler/200810/political-rumors-in-the-2008-election; accessed June 10, 2010.

50 Fight the Smears website, http://www.fightthesmears.com; accessed June 10, 2010.

51 Cass R. Sunstein, *On Rumors: How Falsehoods Spread. Why We Believe Them. What Can Be Done* (New York: Farrar, Straus & Giroux, 2009); reviewed in Elizabeth Kolbert, "The Things People Say," *The New Yorker*, November 2, 2009. See, however, the Harris Poll of 2008 on where adults get their news, in Chapter 3.

52 Lada Adamic and Natalie Glance, "Divided They Blog," 2005; http://www.blogpulse.com/papers/2005/AdamicGlanceBlogWWW.pdf; accessed June 13, 2010.

53 Quoted in Kolbert, "The Things People Say."

54 Chris Cillizza and Dan Balz, "On the Electronic Campaign Trail," *Washington Post*, January 22, 2007, A1.

55 YouTube.com, https://www.youtube.com/watch?v=r90z0PMnKwI, accessed June 30, 2015.

56 Dean quoted in Gary Wolf, "How the Internet Invented Howard Dean," *Wired*, January 2004, http://www.wired.com/wired/archive/12.01/dean.html; accessed June 10, 2010.

57 Jose Antonio Vargas, "Something Just Clicked," *Washington Post*, June 10, 2008.

58 Matthew R. Kerbel, *Netroots: Online Progressives and the Transformation of American Politics* (Boulder: Paradigm Publishers, 2009), 137.

59 Quoted in Ibid.

60 Monte Lutz, *The Social Pulpit: Barack Obama's Social Media Toolkit*, Edelman, 2009, http://www.edelman.com/image/insights/content/Social%20Pulpit%20-%20Barack%20Obamas%20Social%20Media%20Toolkit%201.09.pdf; accessed June 20, 2010.

61 Julie Barko Germany, "The Online Revolution," in Dennis W. Johnson, ed., *Campaigning for President 2008: Strategy and Tactics, New Voices and New Techniques* (New York: Routledge, 2009), 148.

62 Chapman Rackman, "Trickle-Down Technology: The Use of Computing and Network Technology in State Legislative Campaigns," in *Politicking Online*, edited by Panagoupolos, 97–98.

3 Communicating with Voters: The Old Media

Epigraph quotes from Seth Godin, *Permission Marketing* (New York: Simon and Schuster, 1999), 14; Peter Fenn, "The New Media in Political Campaigns: What the Future Holds," in Dennis W. Johnson, ed., *Routledge Handbook of Political Management* (New York: Routledge, 2008), 126; Evan Tracey, "Political Advertising: When More Meant Less," in *Campaigning for President 2012: Strategy and Tactics*, ed. Dennis W. Johnson (New York: Routledge, 2013), 92.

1 On the history of television advertising, see Edwin Diamond and Stephen Bates, *The Spot: The Rise of Political Advertising on Television*, 3rd ed. (Cambridge: MIT Press, 1996); Stephen Ansolabehere, Roy Behr, and Shanto Iyengar, *The Media Game: American Politics in the Television Age* (New York: Macmillan, 1993); Richard Joslyn, *Mass Media and Elections* (New York: Random House, 1984); Montague Kern, *30-Second Politics: Political Advertising in the Eighties* (New York: Praeger, 1989); Kathleen Hall Jamieson, *Packaging the Presidency*, 2nd ed. (New York: Oxford University Press, 1992); and Darrell M. West, *Air Wars: Television Advertising in Election Campaigns, 1952–2008*, 5th ed. (Washington, D.C.: CQ Press, 2010).

2 TVB *Media Comparisons Study 2010: Persons*, http://www.tvb.org/pdf/rcentral/TVB_Media_Comparisons_2010_persons.pdf; accessed June 23, 2010.

3 "Americans Using TV and Internet Together 35% More Than a Year Ago," Nielsenwire, http://blog.nielsen/nielsenwire/online_mobile/threescreen-report-q409/print; accessed June 22, 2010; "TV Viewing Dropping as Digital Use Rises," Broadcast and Cable, May 31, 2015, http://www.broadcastingcable.com/news/currency/tv-viewing-dropping-digital-use-rises/141319; accessed July 6, 2015.

4 Nielsen Company, "Time-shifted TV Up, PC-based Web Down," Nielsen website, http://www.marketingcharts.com/television/timeshifted-tv-up-pc-based-web-down-13190; accessed June 24, 2010; Leichtman Research Group, January 2014, http://www.leichtmanresearch.com/; accessed July 6, 2015.

5 Ross Fadner, "Bewkes Unveils 'TV Everywhere,'" from MediaPost News, March 3, 2009; http://www.mediapost.com/publications/?fa=Articles. printFriendly&art_aid=101366; accessed June 22, 2010.

6 "Broadcast Station Totals as of December 2014," Federal Communications Commission, January 7, 2015, http://transition.fcc.gov/Daily_Releases/ Daily_Business/2015/db0107/ (DOC-331381A1.pdf; accessed July 6, 2015.

7 Frank W. Baker, *Political Campaigns and Political Advertising* (Santa Barbara: Greenwood Press, 2009), 158.

8 "Top 10: HD Radio Penetration," from Radiomagonline; http://radiomagonline. com/digital_radio/hd_radio/top-hd-radio-penetration; accessed June 21, 2010; Michael Barthel, "Newspapers Fact Sheet," Pew Research Center, April 29, 2015; http://www.journalism.org/2015/04/29/newspapers-fact-sheet/; accessed July 6, 2015.

9 Fenn, "The New Media in Political Campaigns," 128.

10 Study cited in Ibid., 129.

11 Parick Ottenhoff, "Politicians Tango with TiVo," *National Journal*, January 24, 2007, from MSNBC website, http://www.msnbc.msn.com/id/16787089/; accessed June 19, 2010.

12 Steve McClellan, "TiVo: Viewers Skip Fewer 'Relevant Ads,'" *Ad Week*, July 30, 2008, http://www.adweek.com/aw/content_display/news/media/ e3ie8eec957b5ed578b6443475272fb8b88; accessed July 19, 2010.

13 Nielsen, "Time-shifted TV Up, PC-based Web Down."

14 Lydia Saad, "TV is American's Main Source for News," Gallup, July 8, 2013, http://www.gallup.com/poll/163412/americans-main-source-news.aspx; accessed August 17, 2015.

15 Franz et al., *Campaign Advertising and American Democracy*, 1, citing data from Nielsen Monitor-Plus.

16 Dennis W. Johnson, *Political Consultants and American Elections*. 3rd ed. (New York: Routledge, 2015), 118.

17 Campaign Media Analysis Group; reprinted in TVB.org Political Databank, "2008 Political Spending Overview," http://www.tvb.org/arc/ politicaldatabank/PDB_Spending_Overview.asp; accessed June 23, 2010; "Mad Money: TV Ads in the 2012 Presidential Campaign," *Washington Post*, Nov. 14, 2012; http://www.washingtonpost.com/wp-srv/special/politics/ track-presidential-campaign-ads-2012/; accessed August 17, 2015.

18 West, *Air Wars*, 32–35.

19 Ariel Levy, "Prodigal Son," *The New Yorker*, June 28, 2010, 54.

20 Baker, *Political Campaigns and Political Advertising*, 95–98.

21 Craig Garthwaite and Tim Moore, "The Role of Celebrity Endorsements in Politics: Oprah, Obama, and the 2008 Democratic Primary," August 2008, University of Maryland website, www.econ.umd.edu/~garthwaite/ celebrityendorsements_garthwaitemoore.pdf; accessed August 15, 2009.

22 From the MTV website, http://www.mtv.com/thinkmtv/chooseorlose/; accessed June 18, 2010.

23 From the Politifact.com website, http://www.politifact.com/trutho-meter/ statements/2008/dec/03/barack-obama/no-mccains-ads-haventall-been-negative;

accessed June 20, 2010. Wisconsin Advertising Project, "Over $15 million Spent in Presidential TV Advertising Since Conclusion of Conventions," September 18, 2008, http://wiscadproject.wisc.edu/wiscads_release_091708.pdf; accessed June 20, 2010. See also Greg Sargent, "McCain Campaign's Ad Spending Now Nearly 100 Percent Devoted to Attack Ads," in Talking Points Memo TPMElectionCentral, http://tpmelectioncentral.talkingpointsmemo.com/2008/10/mccain_campaigns_ad_spending_n.php; accessed June 20, 2010.

24 "2008 General Campaign Television Advertisements," from Political Campaigns, Their Message and Analysis, from the Department of Communication, University of Missouri-Columbia, http://politicalcampaigns.missouri.edu/08PresCampaign/08GeneralTVSpots.html; accessed June 19, 2010.

25 West, *Air Wars*, 67–68.

26 Jody C. Baumgartner, Peter L. Francia, Brad Lockerbie, and Jonathan S. Morris, "Back to Blue? Shifting Tides in the Tar Heel State: Dole vs. Hagan in North Carolina's Senate Race," in Randall E. Adkins and David Dulio, eds., *Cases in Congressional Campaigns: Incumbents Playing Defense* (New York: Routledge, 2010), 207–208.

27 Disclose is an acronym for Democracy Is Strengthened by Casting Light on Spending in Elections. David M. Herszhenhorn, "House Approves Legislation That Mandates the Disclosure of Political Spending," *New York Times*, June 24, 2010.

28 "Mad Money: TV Ads in the 2012 Presidential Campaign."

29 Jennifer Lees-Marshment, *Political Marketing: Principles and Applications* (London: Routledge, 2009), 111.

30 Catherine Needham, "Brand Leaders: Clinton, Blair and the Limitations of the Permanent Campaign," *Political Studies* 53 (2) (2005): 343–361, at 347–348; cited in Lees-Marshment, *Political Marketing*, 112.

31 Regina G. Lawrence and Melody Rose, *Hillary Clinton's Race for the White House: Gender Politics and the Media on the Campaign Trail* (Boulder: Lynne Riener, 2010), 112–115; quote at 114.

32 George Lakoff, *Don't Think of an Elephant! Know Your Values and Frame the Debate* (White River Junction, Vt.: Chelsea Green Publishing, 2004), 4.

33 Frank I. Luntz, *Words That Work: It's Not What You Say, It's What People Hear* (New York: Hyperion, 2006).

34 Carrie Budoff Brown, "Dems Talk Tough on Immigration," *Politico*, June 10, 2010.

35 John Wagner, "This Just In From Channel Faux News," *Washington Post*, June 22, 2010, B1.

36 *Citizens United v. Federal Election Commission*, 558 U.S. 310, January 21, 2010; majority opinion by Justice Anthony Kennedy.

37 *Austin v. Michigan Chamber of Commerce*, 494 U.S. 652 (1990) and *McConnell v. Federal Election Commission*, 540 U.S. 93 (2003).

38 Ben Frumin, "Obama: Supreme Court Ruling 'A Major Victory For Big Oil, Wall Street Banks, Health Insurance Companies'," TPM LiveWire, January 21, 2010, http://tpmlivewire.talkingpointsmemo.com/2010/01/obama-supreme-court-ruling-a-major-victory-for-big-oil-wall-street-bankshealth-insurance-companies.php; accessed May 10, 2010.

39 "Laurence Tribe on Citizens United v. Federal Election Commission," *Harvard Law School News*, January 24, 2010, http://www.law.harvard.edu/news/spotlight/constitutional-law/related/tribe.on.citizens.united.html; accessed March 12, 2010.

40 Johnson, *No Place for Amateurs*, first edition, 29.

41 Michael Cornfield and Lee Rainie, "The Web Era Isn't as New as You Think," *EMT Current News*, November 5, 2006. ElectionMall Technologies, https://info.electionmall.name/e-pressrelease/emt_news.asp?a=5A5; accessed November 8, 2009.

42 Interview with Justin Germany, partner, Craft Media Digital, June 18, 2010. Craft Media Digital is a firm that works for Republican candidates, corporations, and issue advocacy causes. Germany was the director of online media for the McCain for president 2008 campaign.

43 Michael Cornfield, "Game-Changers: New Technology and the 2008 Presidential Election," in Larry J. Sabato, ed., *The Year of Obama: How Barack Obama Won the White House* (New York: Longman, 2010), 215.

44 Viguerie quoted in Todd Meredith, "Open the Envelope," *Campaigns & Elections* (December 2004), 76.

45 Richard Schlackman and Michael Hoffman, "Direct Mail: The Tactical Edge," in Ronald A. Faucheux, ed., *Winning Elections: Political Campaign Management, Strategy & Tactics* (New York: M. Evans, 2003), 340.

46 Liz Chadderdon, president, The Chadderdon Group, Alexandria, Virginia; telephone interview with the author, June 18, 2010.

47 Ibid.

48 Tad Devine, "Paid Media—In an Era of Revolutionary Change," in Richard J. Semiatin, ed., *Campaigns on the Cutting Edge* (Washington, D.C.: CQ Press, 2008), 39.

49 Stephen E. Frantzich, "E-Politics and the 2008 Presidential Campaign," in William J. Crotty, ed., *Winning the Presidency 2008* (Boulder: Paradigm Publishers, 2009), 137.

4 Campaign Dollars: From Soft Money to Dark Money

Epigraph quote from the Center for Responsive Politics, "U.S. Election Will Cost $5.3 Billion, Center for Responsive Politics Predicts," October 22, 2008. Center for Responsive Politics website, http://opensecrets.org/news/2008/10/us-election-will-cost53-billi.html; accessed August 15, 2009. President Barack Obama, State of the Union Address, January 27, 2010; White House website, http://www.whitehouse.gov/thepress-office/remarks-president-state-union-address. The Center for Responsive Politics calculates total spending in presidential elections by taking the sum of Candidate spending, political party spending, 527 organization spending, independent expenditures and communication costs from political action committees, FEC funding of conventions, and host committee fund-raising. OpenSecrets website, http://www.opensecrets.org/bigpicture/cost_methodology.php; accessed June 10, 2010.

1 Campaign Finance Institute and Center for Responsive Politics data, see Vital Statistics on Congress, http://www.brookings.edu/~/media/Research/Files/

Reports/2013/07/vital-statistics-congress-mann-ornstein/Vital-Statistics-Chapter-3-Campaign-Finance-in-Congressional-Elections.pdf?la=en; accessed August 5, 2015.

2 Center for Responsive Politics, "U.S. Election Will Cost $5.3 Billion."
3 Center for Responsive Politics, http://www.opensecrets.org/pres08; accessed August 5, 2015.
4 Center for Responsive Politics, http://www.opensecrets.org/pres12/; accessed August 5, 2015.
5 Zach Holden, "Overview of Campaign Finances, 2011-2012 Elections," May 13, 2014, http://followthemoney.org/research/institute-reports/overview-of-campaign-finances-20112012-elections/; accessed August 5, 2015.
6 Robert L. Hogan, "The Costs of Representation in State Legislatures: Explaining Variations in Campaign Spending," *Social Science Quarterly* 81 (4) (December 2000): 941–956.
7 National Institute on Money in State Politics, available at www.followthemoney.org/database/nationalview.phtml; accessed August 15, 2009. On expenditures by Native American tribes, who spent $425 million on various ballot initiatives, party and candidate support from 2000 through 2008, see Cheryl Schmitt, "Decade Reveals Unintended Results of Law Expanding Tribal Casino Games," *Sacramento Bee*, December 24, 2009.
8 "Election Results: California," *New York Times*, November 3, 2010. National Institute on Money in State Politics, 2009 Campaign Finance Data, available from http://www.followthemoney.org; accessed November 8, 2009. Over the course of his elective political career, Jon Corzine spent more than $131 million of his own money. The former head of the investment firm Goldman Sachs won the U.S. Senate seat from New Jersey in 2000 ($59 million of his own money); he was elected governor of New Jersey in 2005 ($42.4 million), and lost his re-election bid for governor in 2009 ($25.3 million). Only Michael Bloomberg, three term mayor of New York City, has spent more; Bloomberg has spent approximately $255 million of his own money.
9 Linda Casey et al., "An Overview of Campaign Finances, 2009-2010 Elections," National Institute on Money in State Politics, April 12, 2012, http://classic.followthemoney.org/press/ReportView.phtml?=487; accessed August 6, 2015.
10 George F. Will, "A 'Reform' Wisely Rejected," *Washington Post*, January 28, 2010, A25.
11 *Buckley v. Valeo*, 424 U.S. 1 (1976), the U.S. Supreme Court upheld the contributions limits in the 1971 Federal Elections Campaign Act but ruled that there could be no expenditure ceiling on campaigns. Wealthy candidates were now permitted to spend as much as they wanted on their own campaigns.
12 572 U.S. ___ (2014); majority opinion by Roberts, joined by Scalia, Kennedy, and Alito; Thomas concurred; dissenting opinion by Breyer, joined by Ginsburg, Sotomayor, and Kagan.
13 Federal Election Commission, News Release, "FEC Announces Updated Contribution Limits," January 23, 2007. FEC website, http://www.fec.gov/press/press2007/20070123limits.html. At the beginning of each federal election cycle, the FEC uses the price index, provided by the U.S. Department of Labor, to determine the indexed contribution amounts.

14 The relevant section is 26 U.S.C. 527 (e), which states that an organization that is "organized and operated primarily for the purpose of directly or indirectly accepting contributions or making expenditures" did not need to declare contributions, dues or fund-raising proceeds as income if the money is used for "the function of influencing or attempting to influence the selection, nomination, election, or appointment of any individual to any Federal, State, or local public office." See George J. Terwilliger III and John C. Wells, "527 Organizations," *National Law Journal*, September 13, 2004.

15 Public Citizen, *Second Quarter Stockpile: 527 Political Groups Continue Soft Money Grab During 2002 Cycle* (August 13, 2002); http://www.citizen.org/documents/527/527_2ndQ.pdf; accessed November 8, 2009.

16 551 U.S. 449 (2007).

17 Anthony Gierzynski, "The Promise and Futility of American Campaign Financing," in Dennis W. Johnson, ed., *Routledge Handbook of Political Management* (New York: Routledge, 2009), 152.

18 The Campaign Finance Institute, *Soft Money Political Spending by 501(c) Nonprofits Tripled in 2008 Election*, February 25, 2009, http://www.cfinst.org/pr/prRelease.aspx?ReleaseID=221; accessed August 15, 2009.

19 A good summary of federal campaign finance law is Trevor Potter, "The Current State of Campaign Finance Law," in *The New Campaign Finance Sourcebook*, eds. Anthony Corrado, Daniel R. Ortiz, Thomas E. Mann, and Trevor Potter (Washington, D.C.: Brookings Institution, 2005) and Federal Election Commission, *Public Funding of Presidential Elections*, January 2009, http://www.fec.gov/pages/brochures/pubfund.shtml; accessed September 17, 2009.

20 For an analysis of the 2008 presidential campaign financing, see Anthony J. Corrado and Molly Corbett, "Rewriting the Playbook on Presidential Campaign Financing," in Dennis W. Johnson, ed., *Campaigning for President 2008: Strategy and Tactics. New Voices and New Techniques* (New York: Routledge, 2009), 126–146; on the 2012 election, see Anthony Corrado, "The Money Race: A New Era of Unlimited Funding?" in Dennis W. Johnson, ed., *Campaigning for President 2012: Strategy and Tactics* (New York: Routledge, 2013), 59–80.

21 558 U.S. 310 (2010). Kennedy was joined by John Roberts, Antonin Scalia, Samuel Alito, and Clarence Thomas (except for Part IV); John Paul Stevens wrote the dissent, joined by Ruth Bader Ginsburg, Stephen Breyer, and Sonia Sotomayor.

22 Kennedy quote at Ibid., 330–331.

23 Stevens quote at Ibid., 398.

24 Corrado, "The Money Race."

25 *SpeechNow.org v. FEC*, http://www.fec.gov/law/litigation/speechnow.shtml; accessed August 12, 2015.

26 Center for Responsive Politics, "Super PACS."

27 Center for Responsive Politics, "Political Nonprofits (Dark Money)," http://www.opensecrets.org/outsidespending/nonprof_summ.php; accessed August 13, 2015; Editorial, "Dark Money Helped Win the Senate," *New York Times*, November 8, 2014.

28 Jim Drinkard and Laurence McQuillen, "'Bundling' Contributions Pay for Bush Campaign," *USA Today*, October 16, 2003.

29 Public Citizen's website, *WhiteHouseforSale.org*, http://www.whitehouseforsale. org/candidate.cfm?CandidateID=C0009; accessed September 17, 2009.

30 David D. Kirkpatrick, "Use of Bundlers Raises New Risks for Campaigns," *The New York Times*, August 31, 2007.

31 Center for Responsive Politics, "Bundlers," Open Secrets website, http:// www.opensecrets.org/pres12/bundlers.php?id=N00000286&cycle=2012; accessed August 12, 2015.

32 John F. Persinos, "Ollie, Inc.: How Oliver North Raised over $20 Million in a Losing U.S. Senate Race," *Campaigns and Elections*, June 1995, 30.

33 Dennis W. Johnson, *No Place for Amateurs: How Political Consultants Are Reshaping American Democracy* (New York: Routledge, 2001), 161.

34 J. Friedly, "Fund-Raisers Predict Surge in Internet Spending," *The Hill*, March 18, 1998, 1. See also, Ron Faucheux, "How Campaigns Are Using the Internet," *Campaigns and Elections*, September, 1998.

35 Don Van Natta, Jr., "McCain Gets Big Payoff on Web Site," *The New York Times*, February 4, 2000, A24.

36 From Donatelli's political consulting firm, Campaign Solutions website, http:// www.campaignsolutions.com/fundraising.html; accessed May 28, 2010.

37 Gary Wolf, "How the Internet Invented Howard Dean," *Wired*, January 2004, http://www.wired.com/wired/archive/12.01/dean.html; accessed November 8, 2009.

38 Larry Biddle, "Fund-Raising: Hitting Home Runs On and Off the Internet," in Zephyr Teachout and Tom Sweeter, eds., *Mousepads, Shoe Leather, and Hope* (Boulder: Paradigm Publishers, 2008), 170.

39 Garrett M. Graff, "Barack Obama: How Content Management and Web 2.0 Helped Win the White House," *Infonomics*, March–April 2009; the AIIM website, at http://www.aiim.org/Infonomics/Obama-How-Web2.0-Helped-Win-Whitehouse.aspx; accessed May 28, 2010.

40 Jose Antonio Vargas, "Obama Raised Half a Billion Online," *Washington Post*, August 20, 2008.

41 Anthony Corrado and Molly Corbett, "Rewriting the Playbook on Presidential Campaign Financing," in Dennis W. Johnson, ed., *Campaigning for President 2008: Strategy and Tactics, New Voices and New Techniques* (New York: Routledge, 2009), 127.

42 Kenneth P. Vogel, "'Money Bomb': Ron Paul Raises $6 Million in 24-Hour Period," *USA Today*, December 17, 2007.

43 ActBlue website, available at http://actblue.org; accessed April 22, 2010.

44 Slatecard.com website, available at http://www.slatecard.com; accessed April 22, 2010.

45 BlueStateDigital website, available at http://www.bluestatedigital.com; accessed April 22, 2010.

46 Gordon MacMillan, "Blue State Digital Creates TonyBlair4Labour Site," BrandRepublic.com, http://brandrepublic.com/discipline/digitalmarketing/ news/994174/Blue-State-Digital-creates-TonyBlair4Labour-site; accessed April 22, 2010. BSD had developed several other websites for Blair's nonpolitical interests.

47 Delaney quoted in Daniel Newshauser, "Tell Pawlenty What To Do With His Money," *CQ Politics News*, April 24, 2010, http://cqpolitics.com/frame-templates/print_template.html; accessed May 6, 2010.

48 The first to write about "crowdsourcing" was Jeff Howe, "The Rise of Crowdsourcing," *Wired*, June 2006, http://www.wired.com/wired/archive/14.06/crowds.htm; accessed April 21, 2010.

49 Michael J. Malbin and Sean A. Cain, *The Ups and Downs of Small and Large Donors: An Analysis of Pre- and Post-BCRA Contributions to Federal Candidates and Parties. 1999–2006*, Campaign Finance Institute, 2007, 14; http://www.cfinst.org/books_reports/SmallDonors/Small-Large-Donors_June2007.pdf

50 Samantha Sanchez, "Average Contribution Size in State Legislative Races," NIMSP website, http://www.followthemoney.org/pres/ZZ/19990702.phtml; accessed September 17, 2009.

51 Data from Michael McDonald, George Mason University, "2008 General Election Turnout Rates" updated April 26, 2009, http://elections.gmu.edu/Turnout_2008G.html; accessed August 15, 2009.

52 Peter Olsen-Phillips, Russ Choma, Sarah Bryner, and Doug Weber, "The Political One Percent of the One Percent in 2014," April 30, 2015, http://opensecrets.org/news/2015/04/the-political-one-percent-of-the-one-percent; accessed August 13, 2015.

53 Kenneth P. Vogel, Tarini Parti, and Theodoric Meyer, "67 Donors and Gusher of Cash Change 2016 Race," *Politico*, August 1, 2015.

5 Taking the Pulse of the Electorate

Epigraph quote from William R. Hamilton, "Political Polling: From the Beginning to the Center," in James A. Thurber and Candice J. Nelson, eds., *Campaigns and Elections: American Style* (Boulder: Westview, 1995), 178. Telephone interview with Paul Maslin, principal, Fairbank, Maslin, Maullin and Metz (FM3 Research), Madison, Wisconsin, April 16, 2010.

1 Daniel S. Greenberg, "Why Voters Should Just Say No to the Plague of Political Polling," *Chicago Tribune*, October 24, 1990, 19.

2 For a short description and analysis of each survey research technique, see Dennis W. Johnson, *Political Consultants and American Elections: Hired to Fight. Hired to Win* (New York: Routledge, 2016), Chapter 5.

3 National Council on Public Polls, Polling Review Board, "Errors Associated with 'Instant' and Overnight Polls" (2000), http://ncpp.org/instant.htm; accessed May 1, 2001. See, Dennis W. Johnson, "Elections and Public Polling: Will the Media Get Online Polling Right?" *Journal of Psychology and Marketing* 19 (12) (November 2002): 1009–1023.

4 FiveThirtyEight.com was created by Nate Silver; RealClearPolitics.com was created in 2000 by John McIntyre and Tom Bevan; Pollster.com, launched in 2006, is owned by YouGov/Polimetrix, Mark Blumenthal is the editor and publisher and Charles Franklin is the co-developer.

5 Pew Research Center for the People and the Press, "Methodology: Collecting Survey Data," n.d.; http://people-press.org/methodology/collecting/#3; accessed May 28, 2010; Scott Keeter, Courtney Kennedy, Michael Domock, Jonathan Best, Peyton Craighill, "Gauging the Impact of Growing Nonresponse on Estimates from a National RDD Telephone Survey," *Public Opinion Quarterly* 70 (5): 759–779.

6 Public opinion and marketing scholars and others began worrying about the growing refusal rates in the 1970s in consumer surveys. Frederick Wiseman and Philip McDonald, "Noncontact and Refusal Rates in Consumer Telephone Surveys," *Journal of Marketing Research* XVI (November 1979): 478–484.

7 Morris Fiorina and Jon Krosnick, "The Economist/YouGov Internet Presidential Poll," 2004, http://www2.economist.com/media/pdf/paper.pdf; accessed August 15, 2009; Gary Langer, "About Response Rates: Some Unresolved Questions," *Public Perspective* 14 (3) May/June 2003, http://webapps.ropercenter. uconn.edu/ppscan/143/143016.pdf; accessed May 28, 2010.

8 See Candice J. Nelson, "Polling—Trends in the Early Twenty-First Century," in Richard J. Semiatin, ed., *Campaigns on the Cutting Edge* (Washington, D.C.: CQ Press, 2008), 69.

9 Donald P. Green and Alan S. Gerber, "Enough Already with Random Digit Dialing: A Proposal to Use Registration-Based Sampling to Improve Pre-Election Polling," Gallup Conference on Improving the Accuracy of Polling, May 2–4, 2002, Washington, DC.; http://bbs.vcsnet.com/pdf/ RegistrationBasedSampling.pdf; accessed May 28, 2010.

10 Nelson, "Polling—Trends in the Early Twenty-First Century," 72.

11 Telephone interview, David Mermin, partner, Lake Research, San Francisco, CA, April 20, 2010.

12 "Cell Phone Edges Alarm Clock as Most Hated Invention, Yet One We Cannot Live Without," press release, Lemelson-MIT Program, January 21, 2004, http:// web.mit.edu/invent/n-pressreleases/n-press-04index.html, accessed August 15, 2009; Cecelia Kang, "Number of Cellphones Exceeds U.S. Population," *Washington Post*, October 11, 2011, citing CTIA semi-annual survey data, http://www.ctia.org/policy-initiatives/research/index.cfm/AID/10316; accessed July 7, 2015.

13 Peter Leo, "Cell Phone Statistics That May Surprise You," *Pittsburgh Post-Gazette*, March 16, 2006, http://www.post-gazette.com/pg/06075/671034-294.stm; accessed May 28, 2010.

14 Stephen J. Blumberg and Julian V. Luke, "Wireless Substitution: Early Release of Estimates from the National Health Interview Survey, July–December 2009, Centers for Disease Control and Prevention," http://www. cdc.gov/nchs/data/nhis/earlrelease/wireless201005.pdf; accessed May 28, 2010. See also, Leah Christian, Scott Keeter, Kristen Purcell, and Aaron Smith, "Assessing the Cell Phone Challenge," Pew Research Center, May 20, 2010, http://pewresearch.org/pubs/1601/assessing-cell-phone-challengein-public-opinion-surveys; accessed May 28, 2010.

15 Mark Mellman, "Pollsters' Cellphonobia," *The Hill*, May 23, 2007.

16 John Zogby, "Why We Won't Call Cells," *Politics*, September 2008, 64.

17 The Federal Communications Commission (FCC) promulgated a set of regulations (47 CFR 64.1200) that have been interpreted to mean that survey research organizations can never use automatic or mechanical dialers without express consent of those being called. Without that consent, cell phones have to be called manually.

18 Scott Keeter, "How Serious is Polling's Cell-Only Problem?" Pew Research Center Publications (June 20, 2007), http://pewresearch.org/pubs/515/ polling-cell-only-problem; accessed September 17, 2009. Mark Mellman

estimates the costs for manually dialing cell phones to be five to fifteen times higher than RDD; Mellman, "Pollsters' Cellphonobia."

19 Scott Keeter, Courtney Kennedy, April Clark, Trevor Tompson, and Mike Mokrzycki, "What's Missing from National RDD Surveys? The Impact of the Growing Cell-Only Population." Revised version of paper presented at the 2007 annual conference of the American Association for Public Opinion Research, Anaheim, California, May 17–20, http://pewresearch.org/assets/pdf/514.pdf; accessed September 17, 2009.

20 Christian et al., "Assessing the Cell Phone Challenge."

21 Paul J. Lavrakas, Charles D. Shuttles, Charlotte Steeh, and Howard Fienberg, "The State of Surveying Cell Phone Numbers in the United States: 2007 and Beyond," *Public Opinion Quarterly* 71 (5) (2007): 841.

22 AAPOR Cell Phone Task Force, Paul J. Lavrakas, chair, "Guidelines and Considerations for Survey Researchers When Planning and Conducting RDD and Other Telephone Surveys in the U.S. With Respondents Reached via Cell Phone Numbers," April 2008, http://www.aapor.org/uploads/Final_AAPOR_Cell_Phone_TF_report_041208.pdf; accessed September 17, 2009.

23 Ibid. Kasper M. Hansen, "The Effects of Incentives, Interview Length, and Interviewer Response Rates in a CATI-study," *International Journal of Public Opinion Research* 19(1) (2007):112–121.

24 J. Puzzanghera, "Online Polling Experiment Stirs Excitement, Skepticism," *Silicon Valley News*, December 13, 2000.

25 Chris Suellentrop, "Why Online Polls Are Bunk," *Slate*, December 27, 2000.

26 Anna Greenberg and Douglas Rivers, "Pioneer Days: The Promise of Online Polling," April 1, 2001, http://greenbergresearch.com/index.php?ID=979; accessed August 15, 2009.

27 Humphrey Taylor, John Bremer, Cary Overmeyer, Jonathan W. Siegel, and Gerge Terhanian, "The Record of Internet-Based Opinion Polls in Predicting the Results of 72 Races in the November 2000 U.S. Elections," *International Journal of Market Research* 43 (Quarter 2) (2001): 1.

28 Carl Bialik, "Grading the Pollsters," *Wall Street Journal*, November 6, 2006, warns, however, that final victory-loss isn't the only measure of the accuracy of online polls. What was more important was the accuracy of the numbers; he noted that Zogby, for example, while identifying 18 out of 19 Senate winners correctly, was off by 8.6 percentage points in those polls, twice the average of other online polls he examined. Bialik found that telephone-based polls tended to be better than online surveys and that companies using recorded voices rather than live voices did even better.

29 From the YouGov Politmetrix website, December 8, 2006 news release, "Polimetrix and YouGov Enter Strategic Partnership," http://www.polimetrixcom/news/120806; accessed June 3, 2010.

30 Darren Davidson, "YouGov Bang on the Money with U.S. Presidential Election Prediction," *Brand Republic*, November 7, 2008, http://www.brandrepublic.com/News/860495/YouGov-bang-money-US-presidentialelection-prediction; accessed June 5, 2010.

31 R. O'Brien, "Review Board Will Watch, Evaluate Net Polls in 2000," Freedom Forum Online (2000), http://www.freedomforum.org/professional/2000/1/polls.asp. See also, Alan J. Rosenblatt, "On-Line Polling: Methodological

Limitations and Implications for Electronic Democracy," *Harvard International Journal of Press/Politics* 4 (2) (Spring 1999): 30–44.

32 K. Collins, "Will Online Polling Destroy the Survey Business?" Freedom Forum Online (1999); http://www.freedomforum.org/technolgoy/1999/10/1 onlinepolling.asp.

33 Robert P. Berrens, Alok K. Bohara, Hank Jenkins-Smith, Carol Silva, and David L. Weimer, "The Advent of Internet Surveys for Political Research: A Comparison of Telephone and Internet Samples," *Political Analysis* 11 (1) (2003): 1–22.

34 Address-Based Sampling (ABS) data comes from the U.S. Postal Service (USPS) Delivery Sequence File, which contains all delivery point addressed service by the USPS. See Michael W. Link, Michael P. Battaglia, Martin R. Frankel, Larry Osborn, and Ali H. Mokdad, "Comparison of Data Quality from BRFSS Mail and Telephone Surveys" (2005); available from U.S. Office of Management and Budget, Federal Committee on Statistical Methodology website, http://www. fcsm.gov/05papers/Link_Mokdad_etal_IIB.pdf; accessed June 4, 2010.

35 From the Knowledge Networks website, http://www.knowledgenetworks. com/knpanel/index.html; accessed June 4, 2010.

36 Stuart Rothenberg, "It May Look and Smell Like a Poll, But Is It?" *The Rothenberg Political Report*, April 10, 2006, http://rothernbergpoliticalreport. blogspot.com/2006/04/it-may-look-and-smell-like-poll-but-is.html; accessed June 5, 2010. Rothenberg notes that there is the Wall Street Journal Online/ Zogby International online poll. Nate Silver, "Which Polls Fared Best (and Worst) in the 2012 Presidential Race," *New York Times*, November 10, 2012.

37 "U.S. Online MR Gains Drop," *Inside Research* 20 (1) (2009): 11–134. Cited in AAPOR "Report on Online Panels," Reg Baker, chair (March 2010), http:// aapor.org/AM/Template.cfm?Section=AAPOR_Committee_and_Task_ Force_Reports&Template=/CM/ContentDisplay.cfm&ContentID=2223; accessed May 28, 2010.

38 Benenson quoted in Thomas Crampton, "About Online Surveys, Traditional Pollsters Are: (C) Somewhat Disappointed," *New York Times*, May 31, 2007.

39 Maslin interview.

40 Autry quoted in Nelson, "Polling—Trends in the Early Twenty-First Century," 77.

41 Mike O'Neil, "Robo-polls Cheap and Untrustworthy," *Arizona Capitol Times*, May 28, 2010.

42 Jason Horowitz, "Numbers Man Adds Fuel to Political Fire," *Washington Post*, June 17, 2010, C1.

43 Gary C. Jacobson, "The Polls: Polarized Opinion in the States: Partisan Differences in Approval Ratings of Governors, Senators, and George W. Bush," *Presidential Studies Quarterly* 36 (4) (December 2006): 732–757, at 733.

44 Mark Blumenthal "The Case for Robo-Pollsters," *National Journal Online*, September 14, 2009; http://www.nationaljounral.com/njonline/print_ friendly.php?ID=mp_20090911_5838; accessed June 4, 2010. The National Council on Public Polls analysis, http://ncpp.org/files/NCPP_2008_analysis_ of_election_polls_121808%20pdf_0.pdf; AAPOR's analysis, http://aapor. org/uploads/AAPOR_Rept_FINAL-Rev-4-13-09.pdf; and Pew Research

Center's analysis, http://pewresearch.org/pubs/1266/polling-challenges-election-08-success-indealing-with.

45 Blumenthal, "The Case for Robo-Pollsters."

46 Mark Mellman, "Robo-polls and Human Error," *The Hill*, February 2, 2010.

47 From the Victory Enterprises website, http://www.victoryenterprises.com/seven.htm; accessed May 28, 2010.

48 From the Susquehanna Polling and Research website, http://grassrootspa.com/blogcore/pdf/SusquehannaCD12.pdf; accessed May 28, 2010.

49 From the RTNielson website, http://www.rtnielson.com/pages/political.shtml; accessed May 28, 2010. See also, Richard J. Semiatin, *Campaigns in the 21st Century: The Changing Mosaic of American Politics* (Boston: McGraw Hill, 2005), 110.

50 Mister Poll website, http://misterpoll.com; accessed June 5, 2015.

51 From the Pulse Opinion Research website, available at https://www.pulseopinionresearch.com/Surveys; accessed June 5, 2010.

52 PrecisionPolling website, http://www.precisionpolling.com/features/political_campaigns; accessed June 5, 2010.

53 Mark Blumenthal, "Everyone's a Pollster," National Journal Online, January 19, 2010; available at http://www.nationaljournal.com/njonline/mp_20100119_8090.php; accessed June 4, 2010.

6 Voter Identification, Contact, and Mobilization

Epigraph quotes from Hal Malchow, *The New Political Targeting* (Washington, D.C.: Campaigns and Elections Magazine, 2003), 9; Alex Gage in Chris Cillizza, "Romney's Data Cruncher," *Washington Post*, July 5, 2007, A1; and Mark Penn with E. Kinney Zalesne, *Microtrends: The Small Forces Behind Tomorrow's Big Changes* (New York and Boston: Twelve, 2007), xii.

1 Voter Registration, San Mateo County website, http://www.shapethefuture.org/voterregistration/voterfileinfo.asp; accessed May 28, 2010.

2 Department of State, State of Michigan, http://www.michigan.gov/sos/0,1607,7-127-1633_11976_12001-27157—,00.html; accessed May 28, 2010.

3 From Aristotle website, http://www.aristotle.com; accessed May 1, 2010.

4 Ken Strasma, "Microtargeting: New Wave Political Campaigning," Winning Campaigns website, http://winningcampaigns.org/Winning-Campaigns-Archive-Articles/Micro-Targeting-New-Wave-Political-Campaigning.html; accessed May 28, 2010.

5 From advertisements placed by Response Unlimited and the Rich List Company of Leslie Mandel Enterprises, in *Campaigns and Elections*, January 1992, 30–31.

6 Chris Cillizza, "Romney's Data Cruncher," *Washington Post*, July 5, 2007, A1.

7 Penn, *Microtrends*, xv.

8 Hal Malchow, "The Targeting Revolution in Political Direct Contact," *Campaigns and Elections*, June 1997, 36. Further elaboration on CHAID methodology and other targeting techniques, see Malchow, *The New Political Targeting*.

9 Christie Findlay, "MicroWizards," *Politics*, June 2008, 37.

10 TargetPoint Consulting website, available from http://targetpointconsulting. com/pages/products; accessed May 28, 2010.

11 David Wiegel, "Persuading the Right People with Microtargeting," *Campaign and Elections*, February 2006; also, Ron Fournier, Douglas B. Sosnick, and Matthew J. Dowd, *Applebee's America: How Successful Political, Business and Religious Leaders Connect with the New American Community* (New York: Simon & Schuster, 2006).

12 Peter Wallsten and Tom Hamburger, "The GOP Knows You Don't Like Anchovies," *Los Angeles Times*, June 25, 2006.

13 Spotlight Analysis, LLC website, www.spotlightanalysis.com; accessed May 18, 2010.

14 Stephen Baker, "What Data Crunchers Did for Obama," *BusinessWeek*, January 23, 2009.

15 Penn, *Microtrends*, 361.

16 Leslie Wayne, "Democrats Take Page From Their Rival's Playbook," *New York Times*, November 1, 2008.

17 Chris Lehman, "Angry Data Nerds Rain on Democratic Parade," *The New York Observer*, http://www.observer.com/node/36133; accessed May 28, 2010.

18 Strasma quoted in Tom Schaller, "Obama's Top Targeter Bullish on Montana and Worried About Gingrich," FiveThirtyEight website, June 8, 2009, http://www.fivethirtyeight.com/2009/06/obamas-top-targeterbullish-on-montana.html; accessed May 28, 2010.

19 Findlay, "MicroWizards," 37.

20 Strasma quoted in Schaller, "Obama's Top Targeter Bullish on Montana."

21 Julie Germany, "Advances in Campaign Technology," in Dennis W. Johnson, ed., *Campaigning for President 2012: Strategy and Tactics* (New York: Routledge, 2013), 81.

22 Will Robinson, "The Ground War: Importance of Organizing the Field," in James A. Thurber and Candice J. Nelson, eds., *Campaigns and Elections American Style: Transforming American Politics* (Boulder: Westview Press, 2004), 148–152.

23 Jakob Nielsen, "Bush v. Kerry: E-Mail Newsletters Rated," *Alertbox*, available at http://www.useit.com/alertbox/20040920.html; accessed May 28, 2010.

24 Chris Cillizza and Shailagh Murray, "The Man Who Helped Start Huckabee's Roll," *Washington Post*, December 2, 2007, A2.

25 Garrett M. Graff, "How Content Management and Web 2.0 Helped Win the White House," *Infonomics*, March–April 2009, 37–44, http://www.infonomicsmag.com; accessed May 28, 2010; and David Plouffe, *Audacity to Win: The Inside Story and Lessons of Barack Obama's Historic Victory* (New York: Viking, 2009), 37.

26 Allison Dale and Aaron Strauss, "Mobilizing the Mobiles," in Costas Panagopoulos, ed., *Politicking Online: The Transformation of Election Campaign Communications* (New Brunswick: Rutgers University Press, 2009), 152–162 and New Voters Project, "Fact Sheet on Youth Vote and Text Messaging," 2009, http://www.newvotersproject.org/text-messaging; accessed June 25, 2010.

27 Plouffe, *The Audacity to Win*, 38 and Graff, "How Content Management and Web 2.0 Helped Win the White House," 42; Germany, "Advances in Campaign Technology," 89–90.

28 Obama '08: The Official iPhone Application, from the My Barack Obama website, http://my.barack.obama.com/page/content/iphone; accessed May 13, 2010.

29 From the Moonshadow website, http://www.moonshadowmobile.com/ground-game/; accessed May 14, 2010.

30 From the respective company websites: www.raisedigital.com and www.purpleforge.com; Germany, "Advances in Campaign Technology," 88–89; DIRECTV Press Release, "DIRECTV and DISH Revolutionize Political TV Advertising Landscape with Combined Addressable Advertising Platform Reaching 20+ Million Households," January 27, 2014, http://investor.directv.com/press-releases/press-release-details/2014/DIRECTV-and-DISH-Revolutionize-Political-TV-Advertising-Landscape-with-Combined-Addressable-Advertising-Platform-Reaching-20-Million-Households/default.aspx?print=1; accessed June 30, 2014.

31 Jeremy Wright, "Mail-in Ballots Give Oregon Voters Control," *SeattlePI*, November 23, 2004, http://www.seattlepi.com/opinion/2600682_oregon23.html; accessed May 28, 2010; and Bill Bradbury, "Vote-by-Mail: The Real Winner is Democracy," washingtonpost.com, January 1, 2005; http://www.washingtonpost.com/ac2/wp-dyn/A400322004Dec31?language=printer; accessed May 28, 2010. Wright was the Oregon state director of the qualifying and general election effort of the Vote by Mail campaign of 1998; Bradbury was Oregon's Secretary of State.

32 Kate M. Kenski, "No-Excuse Absentee and Early Voting During the 2000 and 2004 Elections: Results from the Annenberg Survey," paper presented at the 2005 annual meeting of the American Political Science Association, Washington, D.C., www.allacademic.com/meta/p41477_index.html); Thad Kousser and Megan Mullin, "Does Voting by Mail Increase Participation? Using Matching to Analyze a Natural Experiment," *Political Analysis* 15 (4) (2007): 428–445; Jon Cohen and Kyle Dopp, "Early Voters Breaking Records," *Washington Post*, October 30, 2008, A1.

33 Interview with Bob Blaemire, conducted by Shannon Prasad, September 15, 2009, PoliticsUnder30.org website, http://www.politicsunder30.org/2009/life-in-politics/political-consulting/campaignmanagement/tracking-voters; accessed May 12, 2010.

34 DuHaime quoted in Michael E. Toner, "The Impact of Federal Election Laws on the 2008 Presidential Election," in Larry J. Sabato, ed., *The Year of Obama: How Barack Obama Won the White House* (New York: Longman, 2010), 161.

35 Lee Rainie, "Robocalls During the 2006 Election," Pew Internet and American Life Project, December 2006; http://www.pewinternet.org/pdf/PIP_Robocalls06.pdf; accessed May 1, 2010.

36 "Robocalls Now Top Type of Campaign Outreach," Pew Research Center for the People and the Press, April 2008; http://pewresearch.org/pubs/785/robocalls-election-2008; accessed May 28, 2010.

37 An excellent summary of robocalls and legislative proposals is Jason C. Miller, "Regulating Robocalls: Are Automated Calls the Sound of, or a Threat to, Democracy?" *Michigan Telecommunications and Technology Law Review* 16 (1) (May 2009): 213–253.

38 Dennis Cauchon, "OnceNovel,'Robocalls'NowMoreofaNuisance,"ABCNews, available at http://www.abcnews.go.com/politics/story?id=4152763& page=1; accessed June 8, 2010.

39 From the PoliticalCalling.com website, http://politicalcalling.com/ technology.html; accessed May 28, 2010.

40 In Dennis W. Johnson, "An Election Like No Other?", 14 in Dennis W. Johnson, ed., *Campaigning for President 2008: Strategy and Tactics, New Voices and New Techniques* (New York: Routledge, 2009).

41 David Whiting, "Politicians' Robocalls Drive Me Nuts," *The Orange County (CA) Register*, June 8, 2010, http://www.ocregister.com/articles/phone-252470-call-political.html; accessed June 10, 2010.

42 Jordan Stringer, "Comment: Criminalizing Voter Suppression: The Necessity of Restoring Legitimacy in Federal Elections and Reversing Disillusionment in Minority Communities," 57 *Emory Law Journal* 57 (2008): 1011. Also, Karl G. Feld, "Push Polls: What Are They?" in Ronald Faucheux, ed., *Winning Elections: Political Campaign Management, Strategy and Tactics* (New York: M. Evans and Company, 2003), 184–189.

43 Data compiled from WinningCalls.com website; http://www.winningcalls. com/statelaws.html.

44 Miller, "Regulating Robocalls," 232.

45 On federal proposals, see U.S. Congress, Congressional Research Service, *Automated Political Telephone Calls ("Robocalls") in Federal Campaigns: Overview and Policy Options*, written by R. Sam Garrett, February 7, 2008.

46 "Stop Political Robocalls," http://www.stoppoliticalcalls.org, accessed April 15, 2010. Shaun Dakin is the founder and chief executive officer of this organization.

47 Donald P. Green and Alan S. Gerber, *Get Out the Vote: How to Increase Voter Turnout*, 2nd ed. (Washington, D.C.: Brookings Institution Press, 2008), 106.

48 Ibid.

49 Shane D'April, "New GOTV Research Irks Some Consultants," *Politics*, April 28, 2008.

50 Marc Ambinder, "SEIU's Data Footprint in 2008," *Atlantic Monthly* online column, Politics, October 6, 2009, http://politics.theatlantic.com/2009/10/ seius_data_footprint_in_2008.php.

51 Dan Balz, "Getting the Votes—And the Kudos," *Washington Post*, January 1, 2003, A17.

52 Thomas B. Edsall and James Grimaldi, "On Nov. 2, GOP Got More Bang For Its Billion," *Washington Post*, December 30, 2004, A1.

53 Thomas B. Edsall, "On Nov. 2, GOP Got More Bang For Its Billion, Analysis Shows," *Washington Post*, December 30, 2004, A1.

54 Erin McPike, "72 Hours is so 5 Years Ago," *Politics* (October 2009), 51.

55 Ibid.

7 Outside Voices

Epigraph quote from Axelrod quoted in Maggie Haberman, "Axelrod Says Ad Buy is $25 Million; Slams Rove and Kochs as Super PAC 'Contract Killers,'"

Politico, May 7, 2012; Service Employees International Union website, available at http://www.seiu.org; accessed June 9, 2010.

1 Martin Hamburger, "Political Advertising, Issue Advocacy, and Our Grim Future," Conference on Political Advertising in Election Campaigns, American University, Washington, D.C., April 17, 1998; on the Capps-Bordonaro campaign, see Dennis W. Johnson, *No Place for Amateurs: How Political Consultants are Reshaping American Democracy*, first edition (New York: Routledge, 2001), 118–121.

2 Kathy Kiely, "Outside Interests Pour $37 Million into N.C. Senate Race," Sunlight Foundation, October 7, 2014, http://sunlightfoundation.com/blog/2014/10/07/outside-interests-pour-37-million-into-n-c-senate-race/; accessed July 27, 2015.

3 Dennis W. Johnson, *Congress Online: Bridging the Gap Between Citizens and Their Representatives* (New York: Routledge, 2004), 33–36.

4 Center for Responsive Politics, OpenSecrets website, available at http://www.opensecrets.org/pacs/lookup2.php?strID=C00341396&cycle=2008; accessed November 6, 2010; 2014 data from http://www.opensecrets.org/pacs/lookup2.php?strID=C00341396&cycle=2014; accessed July 27, 2015.

5 Public Campaign website, available at www.publiccampaign.org.

6 Stephen K. Medvic, "Outside Voices: 527s, Political Parties and Other Non-Candidate Groups," in Dennis W. Johnson, ed., *Campaigning for President 2008: Strategy and Tactics. New Voices and New Techniques* (New York: Routledge, 2009), 189.

7 Center for Responsive Politics, "Top Individual Contributors to 527 Committees, 2004 Election Cycle."

8 From the American Solutions website, available at http://www.americansolutions.com; accessed June 6, 2010, link now defunct. See analysis of American Solutions spending in OpenSecrets.org, http://www.opensecrets.org/527s/527cmtedetail.php?ein=205457079&cycle=2010; accessed August 3, 2015.

9 Jody C. Baumgartner, Peter L. Francia, Brad Lockerbie, and Jonathan S. Morris, "Back to Blue? Shifting Tides in the Tar Heel State: Dole vs. Hagan in North Carolina's Senate Race," in Randall E. Adkins and David Dulio, *Cases in Congressional Campaigns: Incumbents Playing Defense* (New York: Routledge, 2010), 204.

10 "Left, Right Proxies Push on Iraq," *Washington Post*, August 23, 2007. The Democratic Congressional Campaign Committee (DCCC) filed a complaint in April 2008 against the status of Freedom's Watch as a 501(c)(4), arguing that it should be a 527 group instead. The difference: under 501(c)(4), the organization would not have to make public its list of donors. John Bresnahan, "DCCC to Challenge Freedom's Watch Status," *Politico*, April 29, 2008. Three large-dollar donors are Mel Sembler, John Templeton, Jr., and Sheldon G. Adelson.

11 Daniel M. Shea and Stephen K. Medvic, "All Politics is Local … Except When It Isn't: English vs. Dahlkemper in Pennsylvania's Third Congressional District," in *Cases in Congressional Campaigns*, edited by Adkins and Dulio, 172–173.

12 Center for Responsive Politics, http://www.opensecrets.org/527s/527cmtes.php; accessed June 11, 2010.

13 Center for Responsive Politics, http://www.opensecrets.org/527s/527cmtes. php; accessed August 17, 2015.

14 From the Freedom Works websites, http://www.freedomworks.org; accessed June 5, 2010.

15 Chris Cillizza, "Democratic Groups Outspending GOP 2-1 in Massachusetts Special Election," *Washington Post*, January 14, 2010.

16 Peter H. Stone, "Party Allies Raising Millions," *National Journal*, April 17, 2010, http://www.nationaljournal.com/njmagazine/print_friendly. php?ID=nj_20100414_8119; accessed June 10, 2010.

17 Peter H. Stone, "Bush's Brains, Rove + Gillespie Raise GOP Bucks," *National Journal's Under the Influence*, March 31, 2010; http://undertheinfluence. nationaljournal.com/2010/03/big-time-donors-not-so.php; accessed June 10, 2010.

18 Stone, "Party Allies Raising Millions."

19 Denise Roth Barber, "Citizens United v. Federal Elections Commission: The Impact, or Lack Thereof, on State Campaign Finance Law," National Institute on Money in State Politics, March 2, 2010; http://www.followthemoney.org/ press/ReportView.phtml?r=414&PHPSESSID=c35d5956c245ce32cd3c585 78c493f3d; accessed June 3, 2010.

20 Center for Responsive Politics, http://www.opensecrets.org/races/; accessed August 15, 2015.

8 Campaigning in the Next Decade

Epigraph quotes from Jagoda, "Why Political Consultants are so Nervous," in Karen A. B. Jagoda, ed., *About Face: The Dramatic Impact of the Internet on Politics and Advocacy* (e-Voter Institute Press, 2009), 101; Mindy Finn and Patrick Ruffini, "Out of the Wilderness, onto the Web," *Washington Post*, January 24, 2010, B1; Matthew R. Kerbel, *Netroots: Online Progressives and the Transformation of American Politics* (Boulder: Paradigm Publishers, 2009), 5. Rhodes Cook, "Through the Prism of Demographics: America's Political Scene," in Philip Davies and Iwan Morgan, eds., *America's Americans: Population Issues in U.S. Society and Politics* (London: Institute for the Study of the Americas, 2007), 26.

1 Paola Scommegna, "U.S. Growing Bigger, Older, and More Diverse," Population Reference Bureau (April, 2004); available at http://www.prb.org/ Articles/2004/USGrowingBiggerOlderandMoreDiverse.aspx; accessed June 20, 2010, U.S. Census Bureau, "Millennials Outnumber Baby Boomers and Are Far More Diverse, Census Bureau Reports," Press Release, CB15-113, June 25, 2015, http://www.census.gov/newsroom/press-releases/2015/cb15-113.html; accessed July 23, 2015.

2 Cook, "Through the Prism of Demographics," 26.

3 Quoted in Jason Horowitz, "Numbers Man Adds Fuel to Political Fire," *Washington Post*, June 17, 2010, C1.

4 Quoted in Jason Horowitz, "Numbers Man Adds Fuel to Political Fire," *Washington Post*, June 17, 2010, C1. See also, Candice J. Nelson, "Polling— Trends in the Early Twenty-First Century," in Richard J. Semiatin, ed., *Campaigns on the Cutting Edge* (Washington, D.C.: CQ Press, 2008), 81.

5 Maslin interview.
6 David Herbert, "Will Twitter Add a New Wrinkle to Campaign Fundraising?" National Journal.com, April 7, 2009, http://www.nationaljournal.com/njonline/no_20090401_7583.php; accessed June 20, 2010.
7 Peter Wallsten and Tom Hamburger, "The GOP Knows You Don't Like Anchovies," *Los Angeles Times*, June 25, 2006.
8 Amanda Lenhart, "Teens, Cell Phones and Texting," Pew Research Center. April 20, 2010, http://pewresearch.org/pubs/1572/teenscell-phones-text-messages; accessed May 2, 2010. Kaiser Family Foundation, *Daily Media Use Among Children and Teens Up Dramatically From Five Years Ago*, January 20, 2010. Kaiser Family Foundation website, http://www.kff.org/entmedia/entmedia012010nr.cfm; accessed May 2, 2010.
9 Linda Stone, "Beyond Simple Multi-Tasking: Continuous Partial Attention," November 30, 2009, from the Linda Stone blog, http://lindastone.net/2009/11/30/beyond-simple-multi-tasking-continuous-partial-attention/; accessed June 24, 2010.
10 Michael Cornfield and Lee Rainie, "The Web Era Isn't as New as You Think," *EMT Current News*, November 5, 2006. ElectionMall Technologies, https://info.electionmall.name/e-pressrelease/emt_news.asp?a=5A5; accessed November 8, 2009.
11 Jagoda, "Why Political Consultants Are So Nervous."
12 Finn and Ruffini, "Out of the Wilderness, Onto the Web."
13 House Minority Leader John Boehner press release, "House GOP Dominates Twitter, YouTube, Social Media in Congress," January 22, 2010; http://gopleader.gov/News/DocumentSingle.aspx?DocumentID=167478; accessed June 28, 2010.
14 Anne Marie Cox, "John McCain Discovers Technology a Year Too Late," *The Daily Beast* blogsite, http://www.thedailybeast.com/blogsand-stories/2009-03-10/how-john-mccain-became-a-twitter-addict/; accessed June 19, 2010.
15 David A. Dulio, *For Better or Worse? How Political Consultants are Changing Elections in the United States* (Albany: State University of New York Press, 2004), 186.
16 Julie Germany interview, June 18, 2010.
17 Neil Postman, *Amusing Ourselves to Death: Public Discourse in the Age of Show Business* (New York: Penguin, 1986).

Further Reading

Books

Adkins, Randall E. and David A. Dulio. *Cases in Congressional Campaigns: Incumbents Playing Defense.* New York: Routledge, 2010.

Ansolabehere, Stephen and Shanto Iyengar. *Going Negative: How Political Advertisements Shrink and Polarize the Electorate.* New York: Free Press, 1997.

Benoit, William L. *Communication in Political Campaigns.* New York: Peter Lang, 2007.

Bimber, Bruce A. *Information and American Democracy: Technology in the Evolution of Political Power.* New York: Cambridge University Press, 2003.

Bimber, Bruce A. and Richard Davis. *Campaigning Online: The Internet in U.S. Elections.* New York: Oxford University Press, 2003.

Box-Steffensmeier, Janet. *American Elections of 2012.* New York: Routledge, 2013.

Brader, Ted. *Campaigning for Hearts and Minds: How Emotional Appeals in Political Ads Work.* Chicago: University of Chicago Press, 2006.

Burton, Michael John, William J. Miller, and Daniel M. Shea, *Campaign Craft: Strategy, Tactics, and Art of Political Campaign Management.* Fifth edition. Boulder: Praeger, 2015.

Campbell, James E. *The American Campaign: U.S. Presidential Campaigns and the National Vote.* College Station: Texas A&M University Press, 2000.

Cornfield, Michael. *Politics Moves Online: Campaigning and the Internet.* New York: Century Foundation Press, 2004.

Craig, Stephen C., ed. *The Electoral Challenge: Theory Meets Practice.* Washington, D.C.: CQ Press, 2006.

Crotty, William J., ed. *Winning the Presidency 2008.* Boulder, Colo.: Paradigm Publishers, 2009, and *Winning the Presidency 2012* (2013).

Dulio, David A. *For Better or Worse? How Political Consultants are Changing Elections in America.* Albany: State University of New York Press, 2004.

Ellis, Richard J. *Democratic Delusions: The Initiative Process in America.* Lawrence: University Press of Kansas, 2002.

Foot, Kristen A. and Steven M. Schneider. *Web Campaigning.* Cambridge: MIT Press, 2006.

Franz, Michael M., Paul B. Freedman, Kenneth M. Goldstein, and Travis Ridout. *Campaign Advertising and American Democracy.* Philadelphia: Temple University Press, 2008.

Geer, John G. *In Defense of Negativity: Attack Ads in Presidential Campaigns.* Chicago: University of Chicago Press, 2006.

Germany, Julie Barko. *The Politics-to-Go Handbook: A Guide to Using Mobile Technology in Politics.* Washington, D.C.: George Washington University Institute for Politics, Democracy and the Internet, 2005.

Graber, Doris A. *Mass Media and American Politics.* Seventh edition. Washington, D.C.: CQ Press, 2005.

Green, Donald P. and Alan S. Gerber. *Get Out the Vote! How to Increase Voter Turnout.* Second edition. Washington, D.C.: Brookings Institution Press, 2008.

Greenberg, Stanley B. *Dispatches from the War Room: In the Trenches with Five Extraordinary Leaders.* New York: St. Martin's Press, 2009.

Hacker, Kenneth L., ed. *Presidential Candidate Images.* Westport, Conn.: Praeger, 2004.

Herrnson, Paul S. *Congressional Elections: Campaigning for the U.S. Congress.* Upper Saddle River, NJ: Prentice-Hall, 2004.

Hershey, Marjorie Randon and Paul Allen Beck. *Party Politics in America.* Eleventh edition. New York: Longman, 2004.

Jacobson, Gary C. *The Politics of Congressional Elections.* Eighth edition. New York: Pearson, 2013.

Jagoda, Karen A. B., editor and author. *About Face: The Dramatic Impact of the Internet on Politics and Advocacy.* La Jolla, Calif.: e-Voter Institute Press, 2009.

Jamieson, Kathleen Hall. *Everything You Think You Know about Politics ... and Why You're Wrong.* New York: Basic Books, 2000.

Johnson, Dennis W. *Political Consultants and American Elections: Hired to Fight. Hired to Win.* Third edition. New York: Routledge, 2015 (formerly *No Place for Amateurs*).

——— *Democracy for Hire: A History of American Political Consultants* (New York: Oxford University Press, 2016, forthcoming).

——— ed. *Campaigning for President 2008: Strategy and Tactics. New Voices and New Techniques.* New York: Routledge, 2009.

——— *Campaigning for President 2012: Strategy and Tactics.* New York: Routledge, 2013.

——— *Routledge Handbook of Political Management.* New York: Routledge, 2009.

Johnson-Cartree, Karen S. and Gary Copeland. *Inside Political Campaigns: Theory and Practice.* Westport, Conn.: Praeger, 1997.

Kaid, Lynda Lee, ed. *Handbook of Political Communication Research.* Mahwah, N.J.: Lawrence Erlbaum, 2004.

King, Anthony S. *Running Scared: Why America's Politicians Campaign Too Much and Govern Too Little.* New York: Free Press, 1999.

Kolodny, Robin. *Pursuing Majorities: Congressional Campaign Committees in American Politics.* Norman: University of Oklahoma Press, 1998.

Lakoff, George. *Don't Think of an Elephant! Know Your Values and Frame the Debate.* White River Junction, Vt.: Chelsea Green Publishing, 2004.

——— *The Political Brain: Why You Can't Understand 21st-Century American Politics with an 18th-Century Brain.* New York: Viking, 2008.

Lau, Richard R. and Gerald M. Pomper. *Negative Campaigning: An Analysis of U.S. Senate Elections.* Lanham, Md.: Rowman and Littlefield, 2004.

Lees-Marshment, Jennifer. *Political Marketing: Principles and Applications.* London: Routledge, 2009.

Luntz, Frank I. *Words That Work: It's Not What You Say, It's What People Hear.* New York: Hyperion Books, 2006.

Magleby, David B. and Kelly D. Patterson, eds. *The Battle for Congress: Iraq, Scandal, and Campaign Finance in the 2006 Election.* Boulder: Paradigm Publishers, 2008.

Malchow, Hal. *The New Political Targeting.* Washington, D.C.: Campaigns & Elections, 2003.

Medvic, Stephen K. *Political Consultants in U.S. Congressional Campaigns.* Columbus: Ohio State University Press, 2001.

—— ed. *New Directions in Campaigns and Elections.* New York: Routledge, 2011.

Menefee-Libey, David B. *The Triumph of Campaign-Centered Politics.* New York: Chatham House, 2000.

Nelson, Candice, David A. Dulio, and Stephen K. Medvic, eds. *Shades of Gray: Perspectives on Campaign Ethics.* Washington, D.C.: Brookings Institution Press, 2002.

Newman, Bruce I. *The Marketing of the President: Political Marketing as Campaign Strategy.* Thousand Oaks, Calif.: Sage Publications, 1994.

Ornstein, Norman J. and Thomas E. Mann, eds. *The Permanent Campaign and Its Future.* Washington, D.C.: AEI Press, 2000.

Panagopoulos, Costas, ed. *Politicking Online: The Transformation of Election Campaign Communications.* New Brunswick, N.J.: Rutgers University Press, 2009.

Plasser, Fritz with Gunda Plasser. *Global Political Campaigning: A Worldwide Analysis of Campaign Professionals and their Practices.* Westport, Conn.: Praeger, 2002.

Popkin, Samuel L. *The Reasoning Voter: Communication and Persuasion in Presidential Campaigns.* Chicago: University of Chicago Press, 1991.

Reynolds, Glenn. *An Army of Davids: How Markets and Technology Empower Ordinary People to Beat Big Media, Big Government and Other Goliaths.* New York: Thomas Nelson, 2006.

Sabato, Larry J., ed. *The Year of Obama: How Barack Obama Won the White House.* New York: Longman, 2009.

Schoen, Douglas E. *The Power of the Vote: Electing Presidents, Overthrowing Dictators, and Promoting Democracy Around the World.* New York: Harper, 2008.

Semiatin, Richard J. *Campaigns in the 21st Century: The Changing Mosaic of American Politics.* Boston: McGraw Hill, 2005.

—— ed. *Campaigns on the Cutting Edge.* Washington, D.C.: CQ Press, 2008.

Shrum, Robert. *No Excuses: Concessions of a Serial Campaigner.* New York: Simon and Schuster, 2007.

Smith, Daniel A. and Caroline J. Tolbert. *Educated by Initiative: The Effects of Direct Democracy on Citizens and Political Organizations in the American States.* Ann Arbor: University of Michigan Press, 2004.

Steger, Wayne. *Citizens Guide to Presidential Nominations.* New York: Routledge, 2015.

Stonecash, Jeffrey M. *Political Polling: Strategic Information in Campaigns.* Lanham, Md.: Rowman and Littlefield, 2008.

Streb, Matthew, ed. *U.S. Law and Election Politics: Rules of the Game.* New York: Routledge, 2004.

Strother, Raymond D. *Falling Up: How a Redneck Helped Invent Political Consulting.* Baton Rouge: Louisiana University Press, 2003.

Sussman, Gerry. *Global Electioneering: Campaign Consulting. Communications and Corporate Financing.* Lanham, Md.: Rowman and Littlefield, 2005.

Thurber, James A. and Candice J. Nelson. *Campaign Warriors: Political Consultants in Elections.* Washington, D.C. Brookings Institution Press, 2000.

—— *Campaigns and Elections American Style.* Fourth edition. Boulder: Westview Press, 2014.

Thurber, James A., Candice J. Nelson, and David A. Dulio, eds. *Crowded Airwaves: Campaign Advertising in Elections.* Washington, D.C.: Brookings Institution Press, 2000.

Trippi, Joe. *The Revolution will not be Televised: Democracy. The Internet. and The Overthrow of Everything.* New York: Regan Books, 2004.

West, Darrell M. *Air Wars: Television Advertising in Election Campaigns. 1952–2008.* Fifth edition. Washington, D.C.: CQ Press, 2010.

Westen, Drew. *The Political Brain: The Role of Emotion in Deciding the Fate of the Nation.* New York: Public Affairs, 2007.

Williams, Andrew Paul and John C. Tedesco, eds. *The Internet Election: Perspectives on the Web in Campaign 2004.* Lanham, Md.: Rowman & Littlefield, 2006.

Witcover, Jules. *No Way to Pick a President: How Money and Hired Guns Have Debased American Elections.* New York: Routledge, 2001.

Zaller, John R. *The Nature and Origins of Mass Opinion.* Cambridge: Cambridge University Press, 1992.

Selected Politics and Campaign-Oriented Blog Sites

AlterNet http://www.alternet.org
Ben Smith's Blog http://www.politico.com/blogs/bensmith/
Daily KOS http://www.dailykos.com/
Huffington Post http://www.huffingtonpost.com/
Instapundit http://pajamasmedia.com/instapundit/
Michelle Malkin http://michellemalkin.com/
MyDD http://mydd.com/
Newsmax.com http://www.newsmax.com
Pollster.com http://www.pollster.com
Real Clear Politics http://www.realclearpolitics.com/
Redstate.com http://www.redstate.com/
Talking Points Memo http://www.talkingpointsmemo.com/
The Campaign Spot http://www.nationalreview.com/campaign-spot
The Foundry http://blog.heritage.org/
The Monkey Cage http://www.themonkeycage.org/

Blogs from News Sources

Chicago Sun-Times Blogs http://blogs.suntimes.com/
Los Angeles Times Blogs http://www.latimes.com/news/blogs/
Political Hotsheet (CBS News) http://www.cbsnews.com/

Political Punch (ABC News) http://blogs.abcnews.com/politicalpunch/
Political Ticker (CNN) http://politicalticker.blogs.cnn.com
Politics Daily (AOL News) http://www.politicsdaily.com/
Tapped (American Prospect) http://www.prospect.org/csnc/blogs/tapped
The Caucus (New York Times) http://thecaucus.blogs.nytimes.com/
The Corner (National Review) http://corner.nationalreview.com/
The Fix (Washington Post) http://blog.washingtonpost.com/thefix/
The Hill Blogs http://thehill.com/blogs
The Speaker's Lobby (Fox News) http://congress.blogs.foxnews.com/
Washington Monthly http://www.washingtonmonthly.com/
WhoRunsGov http://www.whorunsgov.com/?hpid=partnersites

Index